CW00732349

MOM'S A LAWYER

MOM'S A LAWYER

HOW TO START A FIRM
and
TAKE CONTROL OF YOUR LIFE

Miriam Airington-Fisher

LIONCREST
PUBLISHING

MOM'S A LAWYER

How to Start a Firm and Take Control of Your Life

FIRST EDITION

ISBN   978-1-5445-3706-1 *Hardcover*

978-1-5445-3705-4 *Paperback*

978-1-5445-3704-7 *Ebook*

CONTENTS

INTRODUCTION

THINGS ARE ... NOT GREAT

We may be in the midst of the Great Resignation, but for years, women have already been part of what Harvard economist Cynthia Goldin calls the "Quiet Resignation." Thirty percent of women attorneys leave their profession.[1] A recent study showed that one in four women lawyers is currently considering leaving.[2] This is a huge problem, and not just for women. When women fully participate at all levels of society, everyone benefits. When women leave a profession in significant numbers, it robs the field of their knowledge and expertise. In addition, it reduces women's collective economic and political power. Women are significantly more likely than men to reinvest earnings back into their own families and communities.[3] Even in the happiest of families, women benefit from financial independence (not to mention that families and children benefit from dual incomes). Data suggests that children actually benefit academically when mothers work—and girls, in particular, underperform when they observe and internalize traditional gender roles.[4]

Research has identified several reasons why women leave law. In a comprehensive 2018 report by the American Bar Association, women reported several concerns, including workplace discrimination, sexism, pay disparity, and toxic work environments including long hours and a lack of collegiality.[5] This is not a problem exclusive to mothers. Not all women have or want the same family responsibilities. In fact, many respondents to the ABA study reported frustration that their employers assumed that having children would impact their career.

Women, particularly those with children, are often seen as less committed to their careers, and "mommy-tracked" away from leadership roles. If we may need to stay home with a sick child, how can we lead a company? On the other hand, we are told that if we must work, we need to make it up to our children. We are bombarded with mom-guilt-inducing extortions against screen time and sugar consumption, and with Pinterest boards full of DIY craft projects and sensory bins. We've been trying to cram a square peg into a round hole. We have been expected to minimize the inconvenience of our personal lives to our work lives, and shield our kids from our work lives. We are burning the candle at both ends to work as though we don't have kids, and then to parent as if we don't have jobs. It's a women's issue because men have never had to do it like this. And because men have never had to do it, they are not going to change things to make it easier for us.

It's undeniable that children and home responsibilities weigh heavily in the decision many women make to either leave law or significantly scale back their careers. The peak years women leave law coincide with child-raising years in their thirties and forties.[6] Those important career-building years overlap with the years in which most mothers are likely to have the most demanding responsibilities at home, caring for their young children. About one-third of women take extended time off during these peak years—an average of five years out of the workforce—to have and raise children. In comparison, just over 3 percent of male attorneys take childcare leave.[7]

Women working isn't some new modern phenomenon, and we represent a significant percentage of the US workforce. Yet the numbers show that women are unhappier at work than men. There are many issues specific to different fields, and I want to acknowledge that there are high levels of inequality and unique challenges within different professions, including essential workers and service jobs. Because my focus here is on women lawyers, I am speaking specifically to the challenges facing women in our profession and offering some solutions to those challenges. My mission is to make legal jobs accessible and enjoyable for women. There are enormous hurdles to cross to achieve equality in the workforce as a whole, but my hope is that we can use our relative professional status to promote change from within the legal profession.

WORK-LIFE BALANCE

Society gives us some advice on how to achieve work-life balance. We can simply work while our children nap (I have no personal experience with this, as mine each spent the first two years of their lives wide awake). We can hire nannies, cooks, and housekeepers so we can focus on work. While I'm down with the cook and housekeeper idea, I don't really want to outsource the fun parts, like going to the playground after school. Plus, that gets pricey. Online articles advise on how to negotiate maternity leave, or how to explain to co-workers the need to pump breast milk. When I was pregnant with my first child, an older lawyer mom colleague gave me this advice: "When you're at work, you're at work. When you're home, you're at home. Leave work at work, and leave home at home." Sounds easy on paper, but what happens when you get a call from school during work hours? What happens when school is closed but court is open? What happens when a judge sets a hearing in the middle of spring break?

During the COVID-19 pandemic, major newspapers published several articles on how working moms were drowning in the new pandemic-created responsibilities of childcare, homeschooling, and virtual work. Many commenters angrily responded that it was "their choice" to have kids, and moms needed to "just figure it out." Here are some real comments posted in response to a *New York Times* article calling for assistance to combat burnout among mothers during the pandemic.[8]

The comments blaming parents for having children in the first place:

> Having a kid is not a god-given right but a massive privilege and responsibility. I am sick and tired of seeing children suffer as a result of irresponsible, grown adults.

> How about: enough. Raise your children. Make your choices. Is there anyone left in America not asking for a public handout because of this or that?

The comments blaming moms for working when they should be satisfied with being a mom:

But, why would a mom with the financial wherewithal to mom full time take on additional work that pays? Live in the big house, drive a new, fancy car, download one's kids for most of their waking hours to be raised by someone else, self-fulfillment? Done right, there is nothing more self-fulfilling than being a mom.

There is a point where we have to take responsibility for the lives we have chosen. I know many 'working mothers' who simply want to have it all.

The comment blaming mothers for not raising their children properly and therefore making their own lives harder:

Kids aren't asked to do much of anything in some homes... Investing a small amount of time in teaching a mentally and physically capable child how to complete tasks appropriate for their age decreases the demands on a parent.

These comments are infuriating. Shaming women for *having children* and *working*? Seriously? Having children is how humans continue to be a species. Someone has to do it. And working? That's how most people support themselves and their families. It's also how many of us contribute to society, add value to the world, help others, and generally participate in the economy. The message is clear: *stop wanting so much*. Stop wanting to be able to do work you love, have children, and generally be okay.

At some point I realized: You know what? I *do* want to have it all. I want to have an amazing career, and I want to make money, and I want to have a family. I want to be happy, and not be exhausted and stressed out and generally traumatized just by trying to survive. My aspirations are important, and my happiness is a necessity. My dreams are not secondary to anyone else's, and I don't exist just to take care of other people without regard to my own wants. If "having it all" means having a career and a family, then men *have been* having it all; now it's our turn to get in there, too.

THE SOLUTION

It's on us to fix our own circumstances. The solution is simple: we need more power. We need more money. We need to build companies and set policies and hire ourselves and create a system that recognizes our value and allows us to be excellent at work and at home. We need to be the ones to demand parental leave and to give it to others. We need to be the ones to acknowledge that it's not physically possible to find someone else to watch the kids when school announces a snow day at 7:52 a.m. and the court announces it's operating as usual at 8:07 a.m. We need to ignore others' expectations and discard the mom guilt. We need to build our own table and invite each other to sit there. We need to raise children who see their mothers as happy, successful, fulfilled and present...not martyred, exhausted, and dependent.

Instead of cramming our lives to fit the legal profession, let's build law firms that fit our lives. This process is customizable. Not every woman wants the same things, and not every woman-led law firm will look the same. The gift of entrepreneurship and ownership is that you control the vision. Want to run a small solo practice and work twenty hours a week? Do it. Want to build an empire with dozens of lawyers and multiple offices and make millions? Do it.

I believe entrepreneurship is a woman's ticket to professional and financial independence. It's not enough for women to make it to the tops of companies by playing by the existing rule book. We need to build companies from the ground up that are women-led and women-focused. We need to design workplaces, work schedules, and work policies that allow us to balance our own lives. We need to assert ourselves in external situations to normalize the needs of working moms. Being our own boss and investing in ourselves is the only surefire way to create the lives we want. Money is power, and building wealth through entrepreneurship gives us power and independence.

I wrote this book for lawyers who are moms. I'm not an economist, or a workplace expert, or a politician. I don't have degrees in marketing or finance, just law. I'm a mom, a lawyer, and a business owner. I love practicing law, running a business, and being a mom. I became a lawyer because I wanted to be a lawyer. I'm honored to be a part of a profession that serves in the unique ways we are able to help others. I worked hard and hustled for over a decade, gaining trial experience and knowledge that has made me a confident and creative lawyer. My firm has helped free innocent people from prison, reunited families separated by international borders, and stood up for people who have been abused, persecuted, and discriminated against. I know the value I bring to my work, and I'm not ready to drop out at the top of my game.

I'm on a mission to make the legal profession more accessible—and more rewarding—for working mothers. I believe that for women to achieve equality in the legal profession, we need to fundamentally change the legal profession to make sustainable legal careers available to mothers. I know firsthand how hard it is to build and navigate a successful legal career as a mom, because I'm doing it myself. I first became an accidental entrepreneur as a single mother to an infant. Before having children, I was an ambitious associate attorney at a firm of talented criminal defense lawyers. I loved my job, which involved long days in court, evening visits at the jail, and often going in on weekends to prepare my cases. I felt like I had the career I'd dreamed of years ago while watching courtroom dramas on television with my grandmother. In 2016, I got divorced and became a single mother to a newborn baby girl. Overnight, everything needed to change. I needed and wanted to work, and I loved being a lawyer, but I simply could not continue on in the same way and also take care of my daughter. I fell into entrepreneurship, and over the next six years I got a crash course in running a business and scaled my practice. Today, I run a seven-figure, women-led law firm while raising three kids. I've built up my firm and reimagined my role in a way that allows me to have the freedom and flexibility to spend time with my family and take care of myself. Along the way, I've developed policies and practices to support other working mothers both in my firm and in starting their own firms.

As we build our businesses to serve our needs, we have to make sure we are creating sustainable businesses and opportunities for our fellow women. Working moms know what working moms need, and it's more than breastmilk-pumping breaks. A women-led company should have a structure that meets the needs of working moms and nurtures the unique value we bring to the table. We must set policies that serve us, create healthy and supportive workplaces, and elevate each other professionally and financially. Everyone will benefit from our doing this—moms, non-moms, future-moms...everyone.

This book is a beginner's guide to starting your own law firm. It takes the mystery out of getting from Point A (misery and exhaustion) to Point B (independence and enjoyment). I'll walk you through the concrete steps you need to take to get started, from incorporating your business to renting an office. We'll also discuss best practices for attracting new clients, managing your time, and running your firm so you can maintain that elusive work-life balance.

This is a practical guide with a strong dose of *you got this*. As you go along, I want you to keep in mind your personal goals and a larger goal of reshaping the legal field for ourselves. I want you to want it all, and to realize that you deserve it.

I've also created a complete digital package to complement this book called "Mom's a Lawyer: Law Firm Launch," available at www.momsalawyer.com. It includes resources such as video modules, checklists, templates, and scripts needed to launch and run a law firm.

Are you ready? Let's get started.

CHAPTER 1

REFINING YOUR VISION

Not all women want the same things. Some women are leaning in, gunning for the C-suite. Some women are stepping out to homeschool their kids and raise organic chickens. What about the rest of us in the middle, who want to find a balance? The choices we make may change as opportunities expand, but currently, women are making choices within a framework that forecloses all but a few limited options. Which means there's not much choice at all.

I love the law, and I'm proud to be part of a profession that has the extraordinary ability to serve others who are often in their darkest hours. I didn't go to law school for fun. I wanted to be a lawyer, and I worked hard to achieve that goal. I'm especially proud today to have a law firm of badass women attorneys.

I also love being with my family. I like to pick my kids up after school and take them for ice cream. I like to be the first one to hear their stories about their school day, and laugh around the dinner table, and read their bedtime stories. I love spending our summer afternoons at the pool and our weekends hiking, and going on adventures near and far. I know that my children benefit from my being present, and engaged, and involved. I want to feel rested and balanced, and have date nights with my husband, and have coffee with my mom friends. I know that is important for my physical and mental health, and for the stability and success of our family. While we're at it… I like having nice things and feeling financially secure.

As you start on your journey to building your own law firm, the first and most important step is envisioning what you want your life to be like, and how law fits in.

LIFE AS A LAWYER

The media is awash with stories about miserable lawyers and stressed-out women. A 2021 study revealed that 25 percent of women lawyers surveyed were considering leaving the legal profession because of mental health issues, burnout, or stress. More than 20 percent of the women who responded said they had moderate to severe depression symptoms. Nearly 23 percent of women had moderate to severe anxiety symptoms. The report found that *work-family conflict was the top factor for whether a woman was considering leaving law*.[9] These statistics probably don't surprise you, but they do show that something is very wrong.

Practicing law is inherently stressful. We have an enormous amount of responsibility for people's lives. At best, clients have some problem or hurdle they need help resolving. At worst, clients come to us at the lowest point in their lives, when everything is at stake. Every lawyer has experienced jolting awake at three in the morning to check a deadline on her calendar.

We get panicked voicemails and emails from clients around the clock. Early in my career, when I took a week off to go on my honeymoon, I came back to an angry voicemail from a client who said she "couldn't believe I had done that to [her]." It's not a career typically associated with tranquility. When you add in the stress of balancing work and home, of mom guilt, of imposter syndrome... It can be too much to bear.

On the other hand, life as a lawyer can be incredibly rewarding. Remember why you wanted to be a lawyer. You have a unique skill set that allows you to help transform clients' lives. Whether you defend people charged with crimes, or get compensation for injured people, or help divorcing parents navigate a custody battle, you are doing something important. Maybe you help immigrants become citizens, or give clients peace of mind through estate planning, or work with fellow entrepreneurs to set up their dream businesses. Being a lawyer is a privilege, and you are part of a profession of people who devote their careers to serving others.

The first step is committing to continuing to practice law and understanding what it means in your life. Once you've done that, you should envision your ideal practice.

ENVISION YOUR IDEAL

There are a lot of logistics to take care of, but let's start with the basics: you need to know what you want so you can work toward it. Start working on your vision, and go from there.

You need to think about what kind of work you want your firm to do—and, specifically, who you will serve. It's not as simple as saying "criminal defense" or "estate planning" or "intellectual property." Take some time and really hone your image of what kind of work you want to do.

When you're starting out, it's tempting to say you will take on any work that comes your way. Have you ever heard of "rent law"? You know—taking on anything to pay the rent? Avoid. Put some thought into the types of cases and clients you want to represent. You can revise that over time, and there won't be anything *stopping* you from taking on other cases. But it's important to have a clear vision of your ideal so you know how to market yourself, what resources you need, and what to prioritize in the early days.

There are benefits to having limited offerings in your representation. Handling a select number of case types reduces your necessary resources and your expenses. Having a specific ideal client will lend itself to effective marketing tactics, and developing a reputation for a certain niche helps you become the go-to referral in your circle. Again, this doesn't mean you can't take other cases. It means you are honing your focus on your ideal. Do you want an estate-planning practice that specializes in helping women reframe their estate plan post-divorce? Are you an intellectual property lawyer who focuses on the creative arts? A criminal defense attorney positioned to become the go-to DUI lawyer for your region?

Once you know what kinds of cases you'd like to take, you need to drill down on your ideal client. Having an image of your ideal client will make it easier to reach and serve them, in everything from your social media marketing to your office location, to your case offerings and fees. Here is an exercise to help identify your ideal client: 1) Think of your absolute favorite case type. If you could only do one case type, what would it be? 2) Identify the typical client for that case type and list out some characteristics. For example, if you are that estate planning lawyer focused on helping women post-divorce, your ideal client may be a woman in her forties with two children living in a local suburb. If you're the IP lawyer for creatives, your ideal client may be a city-dweller between the ages of twenty and fifty who frequents the local arts district.

As you are developing your ideal client and case type (which will shape your practice), you should simultaneously think about the lifestyle you want. Starting your own practice is an opportunity to shift your work to fit your personal life. How many hours a week do you want to work? Do you want to go to court? How much money do you want or need to earn? Some case types will involve more court appearances or urgent deadlines, which translates to less flexibility and more stress. If you want to work less and earn more money, you will need to focus on a smaller case load of higher-fee cases. If you want to work virtually and run a high-tech firm, that approach may be more successful with certain client bases. If you want a short commute and plan to open an office close to home, what types of clients will you draw from that geographic location? Use this planning time to think outside the box, and don't limit yourself with thoughts like, "that would never work in my practice area," or "my clients would never go for that."

REINVENT YOURSELF

Your brand new law firm is going to be your baby, and it needs a name. You need a name before you do any of the other legal steps to become an actual business. It could be your last name, a reference to your geographic location, or include your practice area. There are different schools of thought on this topic. On the one hand, using your last name can be boring and doesn't tell prospective clients much about your practice areas or reveal any personality. It can also tie the firm's image closely to you, so that clients always expect you to be their lawyer (which can get dicey as you grow and no longer personally assist every client). On the other hand, it makes it easy for people to find you, and if you've already been practicing in your area, then your business will benefit from your existing reputation.

There is no wrong or right answer. I ultimately decided to commit to my name and market my firm with my identity. I had practiced in my city for several years prior to starting a firm, and so I have many referrals and clients who come to us with the name recognition. I also like to be the "face" of my firm, and I do a lot of personal marketing. We will discuss marketing in another section, but for purposes of naming your firm, go with your gut. The actual name is less important than how you brand and market your business.

> Tip: When you select a name, purchase the domain name for your website before you even register the business. That way you know you have the website you want for your firm.

READY, SET...GO

You did it. You decided to bet on yourself, take matters into your own hands, and create an incredible, fulfilling, happy life for yourself. I am *so* proud of you. Being an entrepreneur is scary, but there is no better investment you can *ever* make than an investment in yourself. Feel those butterflies in your stomach? That's not fear; it's excitement. You have a lot of work to do. Maybe you've already left your job, or maybe you're counting down the days until you can take the leap. Either way, it's time to roll up your sleeves and get to work. You've totally got this. Now comes the fun part.

The next step? Finding a space.

CHAPTER 2

SETTING UP YOUR SPACE

"Do you need to sit down or something?" The building manager looked back anxiously as he led me through the office space. I was 39 weeks pregnant, sweating, with my swollen feet bursting through flip flops as I heaved myself through building after building looking for the right office space. I had a vague notion that I wanted to be downtown. I wanted the most affordable rent I could find, and I had approximately no time to waste. That was how I found my first office, where I happily practiced with wonderful colleagues for several years.

The next time I toured office spaces, I had a detailed list of requirements based on location, configuration, and the needs of my current clientele and team. I narrowed my search to a specific area, identified four buildings to tour, and worked with an agent to negotiate monthly rent, improvements, and lease terms.

Finding the right office can be daunting, but I'll walk you through some considerations so you can feel confident in the space you choose.

TRADITIONAL, VIRTUAL, OR HYBRID?

You'll need to decide, at least initially, whether you want a traditional office setup or a virtual one, or a hybrid (working virtually but using coworking spaces to meet with clients as needed). I'm writing this in 2022, and the past two years have seen a lot of changes across many industries, including law. Prior to 2020, I knew very few attorneys who worked from home through a virtual office. Now, I know several.

In my case, I decided to continue using a traditional office. While we heavily utilize technology for efficiency and client convenience, our consensus both among our team and our clients was that the traditional office was preferable.

Even in a traditional office setting, it is vital to be set up to function virtually—that was one of the lessons of 2020. We offer virtual consultations and meetings, and we receive and store our files electronically. We utilize e-signatures whenever possible, and clients pay online via credit or debit card or bank transfer. However, many clients still prefer to meet in person. Some courts and agencies require wet ink signatures, and we receive a lot of snail mail daily. My team has found that we work more efficiently and more collaboratively at the office. So, we are a traditional office with virtual offerings. Last year, I actually expanded to a larger, newer office with a five-year lease. However, if March 2020 happened all over again, we would be able to go home and run business close to usual with a few tweaks. If you open a traditional office, it's absolutely necessary to consider your ability to continue working virtually if needed.

In the past few years, many industries have been moving in a virtual direction. It is completely possible to run a business virtually from a home office. Although I said above that many of my clients prefer to meet in person, I am also of the opinion that if you build it, they will come. If you want to open a virtual office, and you work through the logistics, you will attract clients who are perfectly happy with virtual-only offerings. All of my recommendations here will apply equally to virtual and traditional offices. For hybrid offices, the same rules generally apply, but having a coworking space for a few hours a week, or as needed, may be the best of both worlds in terms of accommodating client needs and preferences.

CHOOSE YOUR GEOGRAPHIC LOCATION

If you are working completely virtually from home, this is easy. If you are opening a physical office, there are a few factors to consider. In my opinion the most important consideration is proximity to your home and your kids' school. Long commutes suck. They are inconvenient and a huge waste of time and energy. I once commuted almost ninety minutes each way for work. It was awful, and I only lasted three years. Since starting my own practice, I've had two office locations, and both were within fifteen minutes of my home and kids' school. When I lived in the city, I had an office downtown. I could leave my home, drop off my younger kids at nursery school, and be at the office in fifteen minutes. When my family moved to a rural area, I moved my office to a well-known business park at the outskirts of the city. Once again, I can leave my house, stop at the school, and be at my office in about fifteen minutes.

Convenience to clients is a secondary consideration. I've learned you cannot always predict other peoples' preferences. When I first opened an office, I thought being downtown was a no-brainer.

It was a central location close to the courthouses, bank, and post office. You could easily reach it from the downtown expressway, and there was street parking. We were in a historic building. But over time, clients increasingly mentioned the traffic, parking meters, and ever-present construction around our downtown office. When we moved out to the office park, the response was overwhelmingly positive. Access to highways, free parking, and more space won out over the panache of being downtown.

I wouldn't invest in a physical office in the middle of nowhere. But assuming the basic considerations of relative ease of access and parking, I recommend choosing a location that is convenient to you. If you are planning to use a hybrid co-working space, research available locations in your city and apply the same considerations as you would to a traditional office.

FIND YOUR OFFICE

You've decided to open a traditional office, and you have an idea of your desired geographic location. So how do you find the perfect place?

When I first opened an office, I drove around town, looked for "for rent" signs in front of office buildings, called the phone numbers, and set up tours. There is an easier way. When I decided to move my office to a new neighborhood, I worked with an agent. There are commercial rental realtors who can help you find and tour offices, and then negotiate a lease and terms with the landlord. If you have a realtor you like, ask if they have any referrals to a commercial agent. You can also call real estate companies and ask if any of their agents do commercial leases. I cannot overstate how useful it was to work with an agent. After one phone call, he identified several office buildings within my desired area. He told me about average rents and what to expect in the process, and he gave me the inside scoop on which management companies had better reputations in the industry. He set up all of the tours around my schedule, and pointed out things about each building (good and bad). After two appointments where we toured multiple spaces, I easily selected my current office, and my agent negotiated a great rate and move-in terms for me. You don't pay anything out of pocket for an agent—they make a commission from the landlord.

When you are selecting your actual office space, there are a few considerations to keep in mind: one, know your current needs; two, anticipate short- and medium-term needs; and three, give yourself some room to grow. Will you be taking client appointments here? If so, you probably want a small reception area and a private office. Will you be hiring a paralegal right away, or do you plan to have a multi-role support staff position? In either case, your support staff needs a workspace, and you'll need to decide if they get a private office or if you want them to work at the reception desk.

My goal has always been growth, and this book is geared toward growing a practice. So, I prefer to look down the road a bit in assessing my current needs. Most commercial buildings require multi-year leases, so signing a three- or five-year lease on a single tiny office may lead to growing pains in the near future. On the other hand, you don't want to pay for a huge office suite to sit empty. Because this book is designed to help you build a firm, I recommend looking for office suites in your budget with some room to grow. When I really turned my eye toward scaling, I hired three people in one year, and I've hired at least one new person every few months since. I recommend having a space for at least one support staff in your first traditional office, as well as an inviting area for clients. I'll explain my philosophy on creating an inviting office later in the book.

Something to keep in mind when touring offices and negotiating with landlords is flexibility on leases. A tip I learned from my agent is that larger landlords (who own large office buildings or multiple properties in an area) often will allow tenants to change spaces during their lease term as long as both spaces are within their portfolio. If you will have the ability to move to a larger suite in your building—or a nearby building in the landlord's portfolio—during your lease term, it eliminates the need for longer-term strategic planning on office selection. In that scenario, it's even safer to start small and scale as you grow.

When you negotiate terms, make sure the office is up to par when you move in. Unless the office has just been renovated, make sure the landlord paints and replaces the carpeting. Check to make sure all the lighting works properly. Some states have requirements for when landlords paint and carpet, but regardless of state law, you need to ensure that the office is appropriately renovated prior to move-in. Many landlords will make improvements or changes to the layout for multi-year leases. An agent can help navigate this, but keep in mind when touring spaces that you may not be limited to the existing layout. A large, single office can be converted to a reception suite, conference room, and private office with a wall or two. If your landlord doesn't own other properties or doesn't offer this flexibility, understand (and perhaps negotiate additional terms for) early termination or sublease options.

If you are working virtually, your hunt is much easier. However, you still need to decide where in your home you're going to work. I know the COVID-19 pandemic had millions of people working from their bedroom in their pajamas. But in my opinion, that is not a sustainable approach to building a highly profitable law practice. Unless you live alone, I strongly recommend having a legitimate home office. Is it humanly possible to work remotely from the dining room table with kids playing, dogs barking, and the television on? Yes, many of us did just that for a few months back in 2020. Is it a path to wild success in your business? No, it's not. Look where you can set up a home office. Convert a little-used guest room, finish out a loft, or—at an absolute bare minimum—set up a reasonable office corner in your bedroom and establish guidelines about who can enter while you are working. If you are just starting out with a home office but you plan to scale up to a traditional office, still try to set up a reasonable working space, but don't beat yourself up if you don't have a full-blown home office initially. There is nothing wrong with starting small and scaling. In fact, it's smart. Scaling from a virtual to a physical office makes sense because it is a very financially safe way to grow in the beginning.

As you decide on your office space, make intentional decisions that allow room to grow. Starting in a small physical office with a goal of expanding your footprint is smart. However, keep in mind that there is a cost associated with moving offices: one, the actual logistics and cost of moving; two, the time associated with updating addresses, notifying courts and clients, updating your website, and the other details that a move entails; and three, the marketing cost of frequently moving your office and geographic location. When I left my job as an associate and first struck out on my own, I shared a small office suite with two other lawyers and just had one room to myself. A year later, when I hired my first paralegal, she had a little desk next to my desk for the first six months before I scaled up to a larger office suite. If you need to start at home without an ideal working space, use that to motivate you to get your firm to a point *quickly* where you can move to a working space or traditional office. I worked from home for about three months in 2020, and that was more than enough for me. My first month back in the office, my revenue nearly quadrupled.

If you are planning to use a coworking space, select one that meets your needs. You may have to tour a few in your area. If you will be meeting clients there, is there sufficient quiet and privacy? Does it give off professional vibes, or "studying in the student union" vibes? Coworking spaces are definitely acceptable these days, but you still need to keep in mind the first impression you give clients. As lawyers, we also want to be mindful of confidentiality. A client may not feel comfortable discussing her messy divorce in a coworking lounge. Also, consider what the commitment is—does the space offer a month-to-month membership, or do you need to commit to an annual membership?

OFFICE SHARING AND SUBLETTING

I've laid out above the three main options I see for a law firm's location. There are some other options, which are common among lawyers but which I don't necessarily recommend: office sharing and subletting.

If you are already practicing in your area, you likely have friends and colleagues in the local bar. Sometimes, a new solo practitioner will sublet a single office from an existing law firm. Other times, lawyers will share space, even if not affiliated as a firm.

While I know lawyers who have successfully navigated these scenarios, in my opinion, they are not ideal.

Sharing space with other lawyers may hinder your own ability to advertise yourself. A law firm may rent you an office, but what about the signage? It may be confusing to clients to meet with a lawyer who works inside an unrelated law firm, particularly if it is in a different practice area. Furthermore, there are potential complications to your relationship with your landlord firm. What amenities are shared? If your practice areas overlap (and you are essentially competitors) how will you handle walk-ins or cold calls? Finally, how will you protect confidentiality and avoid conflicts of interest? Your state bar will have rules about protecting privileged information and avoiding conflicts, which can get dicey if you are sharing office space with someone outside of your own firm.

For all of these reasons, I recommend beginning with one of my three options above, and scaling between them as appropriate. Having your own space for your business has a lot of advantages, and utilizing one of those three options really negates any need to share space with another practice.

THE NITTY-GRITTY DETAILS

Once you have your office space picked out, there are still some logistics to take care of. How are you going to run your firm? If you have always worked for a firm or agency, chances are you had very little to do with designing or maintaining their systems and utilities. Here are some basic systems you need to have in place on Day One.

INTERNET

The most important utility in your firm is Internet access. Most landlords will include the other utilities, but you need to set up a business Internet account. There's nothing special about it; it's just as annoying and frustrating as setting up a residential account. Do this early, as soon as you know when you will have access to your office. Sometimes, there are issues that require the Internet provider to make multiple trips. Sometimes, a building or management company has restrictions on which providers can access the building. I don't really know why; I just know it has always been a pain to set up the Internet in my offices. Don't worry about the Internet/phone packages, because you're going to use Internet-based phones. All you need from them is the best possible Internet, and you need it on Day One, so hop on it as soon as you have a space.

COMPUTERS

I started my firm with my personal laptop. If you are starting out small, whatever laptop you are using now for personal use is going to be fine for Day One. The most important thing is that you are able to connect to the Internet, because you need that for just about everything. If you begin scaling your business with virtual employees or contractors, they may have their own computers as part of the contract. If not, or if you begin with an in-office employee, I suggest beginning with a laptop. In the early days, you may want more mobility and flexibility out of your first one or two employees. As you grow, or once you are established in a physical office, you may consider adding desktops. All of my firm members have desktops because the large screen is easier to use. Attorneys also have laptops to take to court and meetings outside the office, and for working after hours. In addition, we have a few laptops for the office staff to use as needed.

PRINTERS/SCANNERS

Depending on your practice, the most basic printer may serve you just fine. If you anticipate being fully paperless with tech-savvy clients, or you are in a tech-forward jurisdiction, you may not need a printer. I would probably plan to have at least a very basic one for contingencies. In my firm's practice areas, we need to scan and print regularly. Although *we* are paperless, we often receive large files from clients or courts, which we need to scan and save into our system. We also work in various jurisdictions that require hard copies of filings.

Don't go overboard on a printer/copier, especially in the beginning. Large commercial photocopiers are extremely expensive to buy or rent. I've heard of offices paying thousands of dollars per month to *rent* one of those giant machines. There are office-grade printers available on Amazon for a few hundred dollars. If, like our firm, you will be receiving paperwork (for example, financial or medical records from clients, or old files from previous proceedings), I strongly recommend a stand-alone high-speed scanner. We've used a ScanSnap scanner for years, and it was an amazing investment that cost only a few hundred dollars.

PHONES

People need to be able to call your business. The way your calls are answered is one of the very first opportunities to make an impression on a potential client. I recommend starting very early with a clear delineation between office calls and personal calls. Do not give people your cell phone number. Even if you are a true solo right now, you will regret it down the road. In fifteen years, you will get a random text from a former client on Christmas Eve saying "can u call me right now it's important."

Landlines are technically still an option, but I'm not sure why you would use one. An Internet-based provider is the way to go. VOIP (voice over internet protocol) means you can make calls over the Internet rather than a phone line. There are many companies who offer this. I have used Dialpad for years. You open an account with a company and select a main number. This is now your business number that people will call. You download the Dialpad app onto any device—cell phone, tablet, computer—and calls can be answered through that device. Most of my staff answer calls through their computers. I have the app on my phone. Callers dial your office number, but you receive the call on a device of your choice. As the account administrator, you can add additional users as you hire more people. You can also reroute calls at any point. For example, calls to my office go to my receptionist. If she is out sick, she can log on and route calls to my case manager for the day. This also means that if an emergency call comes in (or if I have a phone consultation scheduled but decide to take the day off), my office can forward the call directly to my cell. Furthermore, I can place calls from my cell, but they appear to come from the office number. Team members can work remotely if needed. It looks professional and consistent for all office calls to be originating from the main office number. This program is very, very inexpensive. All you need is the Internet.

FAX

Sigh. Somehow, there are still places using fax machines. In my area, it's usually courthouses. My impression is that this varies greatly by state. When I was in law school seventeen years ago in Florida, most things were filed electronically. The federal court filing system is almost entirely electronic. In Virginia, many local courts require original filing with wet ink signatures (couriers are still actually a thing). We also have some courts and government agencies who send and receive faxes. I actually don't know if fax machines are still being manufactured, but if you want the ability to receive faxes, you can use an app like HelloFax, which lets you send and receive faxes without an actual fax machine. You scan or upload a document and send it in an email, and HelloFax converts the email to a fax transmission to the recipient. This is very low cost, and if you work in a state where fax machines still exist, it's worth it to at least have a fax number. Do not buy a fax machine (if doing so is even possible). Don't be part of the problem.

Okay, so setting up your utilities isn't the most exciting aspect of entrepreneurship, but it is necessary. Now you have the basic tools in place to have a functioning office. Good work! Next, we will handle some of the legal details to get an entity set up.

CHAPTER 3

HANDLING THE DETAILS

You've selected an office space. You've chosen your business name. Now it's time to become an actual business, get a business license, and get ready to open your doors. None of this is glamorous or exciting, but it's essential to have everything in order on Day One so that you're ready to get to work for your clients.

GET LEGAL

When you're a lawyer, everyone assumes you know about all the laws. Every time I've closed on a house, the closing agent has said something like, "You probably know all about this stuff, being a lawyer!" before handing me three thousand pages of nonsense to sign. Personally, when I need to handle a legal issue that is outside of my own practice areas, I prefer to hire an attorney to help me. I hired a small business attorney to set up my firm, register us with the state, and serve as our registered agent.

If you practice business law, you may be well equipped to set up your own entity. If not, just hire a lawyer to set up your registration, federal tax identification, articles of organization, and any other documents required in your state to be legit. Keep in mind that some states have special rules for a professional law office—so either look them up or consult with a lawyer who can assist you in the process.

CHOOSING AN ENTITY TYPE

Step One is to decide what kind of entity you will be. This is an area where I personally consulted with attorneys. Even though I myself am an attorney, I am neither a business lawyer nor a tax lawyer. There are different options for business types, with pros and cons and tax implications. A consultation with a local small business lawyer—and a conversation with a small business accountant—will be worthwhile. The main different types of business entities are: 1) a sole proprietorship; 2) a partnership; 3) a limited liability corporation; 4) a corporation; and 5) an S-corporation. Your business structure will have tax implications and affect your level of liability. You will most likely be choosing between a corporation, an S-corp, or an LLC. Under these structures, owners are not personally liable to the business, so your personal assets are safe from lawsuits or business bankruptcy. Profits are taxed differently based on entity type. More detailed information is available at www.irs.gov, but this is an overview of the likely entity types you will be choosing from for your law firm.

LLC: An LLC protects your personal assets from liability. Profits and losses can get passed through to your personal income without facing corporate taxes. Members of an LLC are considered self-employed and must pay self-employment tax contributions toward Medicare and Social Security.

Corporation: A corporation is a legal entity that is separate from its owner. Corporations can make a profit, be taxed, and be held legally liable. Corporations pay income tax on their profits. In some cases, corporate profits are taxed twice—first, when the company makes a profit, and again when dividends are paid to shareholders on their personal tax returns.

S-Corp: An S-corp is a special type of corporation designed to avoid the double taxation drawback of regular corporations. Profits, and some losses, can be passed through directly to owners' personal income without ever being subject to corporate tax rates. S-corps have special eligibility and filing requirements and need to be registered separately with the IRS. I registered my firm as an S-corp, because of the liability protection and tax advantages.

There is a long history in the legal profession of a bunch of lawyers getting together and opening a firm under a list of last names. Resist the urge to join forces with a few friends or colleagues. I encourage you to start your practice on your own. The first law practice I started was a partnership with other lawyers I personally and professionally trusted. They are excellent lawyers and friends. However, after a few years, I realized I needed to branch off into a solo entity. There was no dispute or disagreement. I simply needed the freedom to be in control and follow and execute my own vision for my business. I want you to create a vision for your perfect life and perfect practice, build it, and then grow it. No one is going to have the exact same vision as you, and so any partnership is going to require you to compromise. No more compromising. We are changing the legal field by building our own businesses that work for us, and then paving the way for other women to either do the same, or enjoy the fruits of our labor. Put yourself at the wheel of your own dream.

REGISTERING YOUR BUSINESS

Your state laws will govern what you need to do to register. You will likely need Articles of Incorporation and to register with the State Corporation Commission with a registered agent. You will need to apply for a federal tax identification number (FEIN) from the Internal Revenue Service. And finally, you will need a business license in the locality where your office will be located. Usually, a small business lawyer will offer all of these services and monitor your annual renewal. You will probably need to prepay some estimated taxes on your business license. You may also need to provide some information from your landlord, including a certificate of occupancy to show that your office is in a building zoned for professional or commercial use. Contact your city hall or visit their website for information on the specifics in your area. My first office was in a city that required in-person application at city hall. My current office is in a county that made the process pretty easy with online forms.

These are all things that need to be done before you open your doors, so I recommend starting this process as early as possible. If a life event is pushing you into the process more quickly, just do the best you can and be aware that there may be some penalties associated with late filing.

GET INSURED

To operate a law office, you need insurance. Here are a few types of insurance you should consider before opening your practice.

MALPRACTICE INSURANCE

One type you will definitely need is malpractice insurance. I have always found this to be an easy and relatively affordable type of insurance. Contact your state bar to find out if they have any referral partners, or talk to local colleagues. There are large national companies like Minnesota Lawyers Mutual and ALPS, which I have found to be very reasonable and user-friendly. If you are starting from the ground up, talk to an agent about your needs. If you're leaving another firm or organization to start your own firm, make sure you understand when your old coverage ends, and if there is any "tail coverage" between policies. Depending on your prior employer's policy, you want to ensure you are covered for any claims that arise from actions during your prior employment, which can come out years later depending on your state statute of limitation. Malpractice insurance really isn't scary at all, but you definitely need it in place before you take on clients.

PREMISE/GENERAL LIABILITY INSURANCE

You will want some kind of insurance policy to cover your office and business property. Some landlords may offer coverage. If not (or if you want more coverage), you can look at commercial tenant policies. Some landlords (like mine) require specific amounts of general liability coverage. If you have an agent you use for personal auto or homeowners insurance, I would ask them about commercial general liability. They may offer it, and if not, they may partner with another company or can refer you to the right place. Umbrella policies are pretty common, as well. As with most forms of insurance, the turnaround time to get a quote and get insured is quick. Ask your landlord for information on what their policy covers, and compare with a quote for your business to make sure there is appropriate coverage. Again, in my experience, this is not a significant cost.

WORKERS' COMPENSATION INSURANCE

This insurance covers work-related injury or illness. I have found the easiest way to add workers' comp insurance is through my payroll administrator, Gusto. I will talk more about payroll in the finance section, but check your state employment commission website for any guidance about workers' compensation insurance laws. These days, a lot of applications have integration, meaning you can enroll in workers' comp insurance (and other benefits) through your payroll company. This type of insurance is very low cost, and you should inquire about it if you are hiring employees. Note: this is not the same as unemployment insurance, which is mandatory and governed by state law.

AUTO INSURANCE

If you are planning to use your vehicle as a work vehicle, you will need a commercial auto insurance policy. It is similar to a regular auto insurance policy, but likely a little more expensive. Talk to your accountant about the ins and outs of claiming your vehicle as a work vehicle based on your use. If you are planning to designate it as a work vehicle, ask your regular auto insurer for a commercial policy quote. You can also get a quote from the company providing your general liability insurance. Keep in mind that the insurance company may require your vehicle to be titled or re-titled in the business name in order to obtain a commercial policy. Having a work vehicle is not a requirement, and it's something that can be done down the road with help from your CPA if you are eligible and if it would be tax advantageous.

SYSTEMS AND PLATFORMS

Before you open your doors, you also need to have some systems in place to make sure that your new firm runs smoothly and professionally.

EMAIL

You need a work email that looks like it comes from a real office. Not your law school email address, not a Gmail address, and *definitely* not reallawyer@aol.com. Use the same domain as your website. My website is www.airingtonlaw.com, and my email address is mairington@airingtonlaw.com. Everyone who works with me has the email address First Initial/Last name @airingtonlaw.com. Google and Gmail make this incredibly easy, and it's only a few dollars per user per month. You will have a professional email address and synced calendar, and you can add employees seamlessly as you scale.

In addition to your individual email, I recommend having an administrative account like office@ or clients@. This may not seem important now, but as you grow, you will have other people monitoring email—and you want emails to go to them, not to you. In the meantime, if it is just you, you can have the office account routed to you. When you hire support staff, you can easily reroute it to them. In addition to the obvious benefits of having support staff monitor emails, it also helps keep messages organized and gives a professional impression.

BANK ACCOUNTS

To open bank accounts, you will need some of your legal documents, including the corporate formation and a letter from the IRS with your tax identification number. For starters, you need an operating account and an escrow account. Check your state bar rules for escrow accounts, as they do vary by state. In Virginia, we have escrow accounts called IOLTAs (Interest on Lawyers' Trust Accounts) which are special accounts where the interest earned goes to a legal aid fund. In my experience, banks are not always familiar with these, so you must be prepared to explain what you need and not just rely on the bank. You will want the ability to transfer between the accounts, and you'll need checkbooks and deposit tickets for each. I only have a debit card for my operating account. Depending on your area, you might not use many checks. In Virginia (remember, some of our courts still use *faxes*), I have occasion to write checks for filing fees and things like that, so we do actually need physical checkbooks.

At the early stage, I would not worry about firm credit cards. I am personally fairly debt-averse, but I know many lawyers use firm credit cards. If you decide to establish a business credit line, be mindful of racking up debt before you open your doors. I would keep it simple in the early days; build up an operating account and cash flow your starting expenses to see how your revenue goes in the beginning.

CASE MANAGEMENT SYSTEM

You need a case management system. Even if you don't have a single client when you open your doors, if you follow this guide, you will soon; and you need a good system to manage clients, monitor cases, and track payments. Clio is a very popular client management system for lawyers, and I use it at my firm. You need a system designed for lawyers so you can be compliant with client trust requirements and reconciliations. Other bookkeeping programs may not be designed for trust accounting.

When you select a case management software, make sure you take advantage of the free training call they offer and watch the videos. I had Clio for a while before I realized there were many extremely useful functions that I wasn't even using.

Another benefit to Clio is that it integrates with LawPay, a payment processor specifically for lawyers. You need a system in place *now* to keep clients, matters, and payments organized. Clio also has numerous functions to run reports which will be incredibly useful to you as you grow. I can't recommend enough that you start using a case management system even before you establish your client list. You need to have a client and case list in a proper system as you grow.

A case management system is key. You need to have client contacts and files organized. You want to be able to run conflict checks, track deadlines, and log payments. You also want to be able to add additional users as you grow your practice.

PAYMENT PROCESSOR

On Day One, you need to be prepared to accept payments. It's insane for a business to not accept credit and debit cards. Make it as easy as possible for clients to pay you. You can accept cash and checks, too. But most people pay with credit or debit cards. Even people without them will often use prepaid cards. Note: you are depositing any and all payments into the proper bank account, and logging them, regardless of method of payment.

There are various card processors, and you can shop around rates, but I have found LawPay the most convenient because it integrates with Clio and allows for delineation between trust and operating. A law firm needs the capacity to take payments into escrow, and not all card processors offer that option. Again, you need to be set up to seamlessly take a payment on your first call. Do the free training and make sure you know how to take and log payments—the more automated, the better. We use LawPay to send clients payment links. My operations manager gets instant notification of payments, and our clients receive an instant receipt confirmation. No excuses, set this up before you open.

Note: I do not charge a credit card processing fee. It's annoying to consumers and an additional bookkeeping headache for me. As I'll elaborate on in the section on fees, processing payments is a business cost that will factor into your overall decision on setting your fees.

SCHEDULING APPS

There are several apps that make scheduling very easy. If you're just starting out, you may not be overwhelmed by scheduling appointments. However, even if it's just you and very few clients, how you spend every minute of your time is important. Time saved on administrative tasks is time you can spend on generating new business. So, automating scheduling, even if it's not yet a time burden, is a good idea. This also ties into the theme of making it as easy as humanly possible for any and all potential clients to get on your calendar.

Two well-known programs are Calendly and Acuity. You can set your schedule based on when you are available to take consultations, or sync it to your existing calendar. You can personalize the homepage with your business information and create different appointment types for people to book, with links to pay for consultations—for example, "Initial Consultation: $250" or "30-minute call for existing clients." You can also embed the software on your website so people can schedule consultations with you around the clock. Just be mindful of setting the parameters, and make some appointments subject to your confirmation so that your calendar doesn't fill up with meetings you don't want. Once you hire support staff, you can turn over the management of the scheduling app to another person.

I find that many people still prefer to call and schedule a consultation. While I am all about automating as much as possible, I do recommend offering multiple ways for someone to book with you. In other words, if someone calls in to schedule, schedule them. Don't say, "go on my website and follow the link," or email them your scheduling link. In the beginning, you want to nurture leads carefully and build up business. As you scale, you will have full-time support staff to do so. Again: we are making it as easy as possible for people to find you, book with you, hire you, and pay you. Never act like you are (or your firm is) too busy to personally serve potential and existing clients.

Now you have the basic systems in place to communicate, schedule clients, and accept payments. You have a case management system to keep clients and matters organized. You have the systems in place to take on clients and process fees. It's time to refine the details of what your day-to-day will look like.

CHAPTER 4

MANAGING YOUR SCHEDULE

We've been working in a system that was never designed to allow us to excel. Despite the fact that women have always worked, the work week and work days completely ignore the reality of family life, especially when we take into consideration the fact that 67 percent of lawyers work more than forty hours a week.[10]

Balancing work and family shouldn't be a women's problem, but that's largely what it is at the moment. In 2017, a Pew Research Center report found moms did more than twice as much child care as dads in the US[11] This tension is not a secret. Everyone knows it's basically impossible to work full-time and raise a family. The image of a stressed out, exhausted mom has become a cultural trope. When I was growing up, we saw it in movies like the 1982 classic *E.T.*, where the frazzled working mom was so busy driving off in her station wagon she didn't realize her poor latchkey kids had moved an alien into the house. Today, we're bombarded by the image of the sleep-deprived mom with milk stains on her suit jacket who hustles by day and drinks rosé by night. Cue the rise of "mommy wine culture" which promotes the idea that moms need to drink to cope with the stressful demands of their lives. According to the American Bar Association, there's some truth to that stereotype. Among lawyers surveyed, more than half of the women screened positive for risky drinking behaviors.[12] A 2016 study found that mothers have significantly higher work-family guilt and work-interfering-with-family guilt relative to fathers.[13]

Now, I do *not* believe family responsibilities belong to us alone. Men need to get it together, like, now. I want to see equal partnership in homes and families, and we should be expecting that level of participation. But we do need to start first by tackling reality, and not all working moms have partners.

I began my journey into legal entrepreneurship in 2016 when I got divorced and became a single mom to a newborn baby. Suddenly, working late nights and weekends wasn't just difficult, it was impossible. I had no choice but to limit my work hours to daycare hours. If daycare was open from seven thirty in the morning to five in the evening, that meant I could work weekdays from eight to four thirty. Staying late for a client meeting or going in on a Saturday to prepare for a trial was no longer an option. Even getting to court by eight thirty in the morning was a stretch, and many evenings I squealed into the daycare parking lot one minute to close. It was incredibly stressful, and even though I had started my own firm and technically was my own boss, I still had external factors to answer to and struggled to make the whole thing work *and* earn a living. Today, I have a spouse who shares childcare responsibilities for our blended family of three kids, but we still face the logistical challenges familiar to all working parents.

The reality is, a traditional forty-hour work week doesn't actually *work* for parents. How can you be at the office from nine to five, when school lets out at three? Who cares for the kids during winter break and spring break (not to mention summer vacation), when your job only gives you two weeks off all year? How many sick days do you need to get through a baby's first year of ear infections and random fevers? Who watches the kids when it's a snow day but the court is open? Lower-income women are exponentially burdened by these demands, but even among professionals with higher incomes, the financial ability to hire a babysitter doesn't cure these challenges.

The actual daily *logistics* of working and having children is just the tip of the iceberg. What about having quality time as a family to enjoy weekends and take vacations? These are serious concerns, brought to you by a woman who once schlepped a baby to court in a snowstorm and parked the stroller next to the counsel table. I've been there, and done it, and it sucked. Let's change it.

KEEPING A CONSISTENT SCHEDULE

Now you're the boss, and you are going to create your own schedule. Anyone who's ever run a business knows it's not all fun and games. Being your own boss doesn't necessarily mean sleeping until noon. There's that pesky part where you need to earn money. No one else is sending you a paycheck anymore, because you're the one writing the paychecks these days.

Think about your ideal schedule. Write down the things you would like to accomplish in a day, outside of work. Maybe one hour of exercise? An hour at the park after school? What bedtime and wake-up time leave you feeling most rested and energized? I'm a morning person, which has helped me survive having multiple small children who have historically adopted a "we ride at dawn" approach to life. If your genius peaks at midnight and you can sleep until nine in the morning, do that. Just write out what an ideal day would look like to you. That's an ideal work day. We do still need to work. My ideal day would be watching the sunrise over coffee, reading a book for hours, getting a massage, taking a nap, and then drinking champagne. If I figure out how to earn a living doing those things, I promise to write another book. The good news is, we are going to maximize the work days, so you can actually have some days like that.

If you're having any creeping thoughts of "that wouldn't work for me," put them to bed immediately. Yes, you have a lot on your plate. No, you're not uniquely busier than other working women or moms. We all have similar struggles. Maybe you are a single mom (like I was when I started my law firm), maybe you feel financial stress (been there, done that), maybe your partner works long hours or travels (been there, done that), maybe your practice requires you to travel, go to court, or adhere to external scheduling demands (also been there, also done that). Adopt the mindset that you can do this—you actually already are, so you might as well do it well and enjoy it.

I wrote this book primarily in the early mornings, rising at four to write for about two hours before my family would start waking up. I typically wake up super early to get a few hours of work in while the house is quiet and I have a pot of coffee to myself. At about six thirty, I start packing lunches, getting the kids ready for school, and getting myself ready. I'm at the office by nine, and I work until two thirty in the afternoon when I leave and pick my kids up from school.

It's important that I have reliable hours at the office to be present for my team, schedule meetings with other professionals during the work day, and be available for client meetings during normal business hours. Being a business owner doesn't mean you float in and out of your office whenever. When you are creating your ideal schedule, I recommend setting consistent office hours. Flexibility within your schedule can still be (and should be) predictable for the people who rely on you, which includes your employees and clients.

Let's look at my schedule again. When you add it up, that's two and a half hours in the early morning at home, and five and a half hours at the office. I may spend another hour on my laptop after the kids go to bed, following up on emails and tasks, but I'm not a night owl and often I just read and go to bed. So that's my eight- or nine-hour workday, but it's scheduled in a way that works with my family responsibilities and personal circadian rhythms.

I typically do not "work" on Fridays, which is a day I use for personal appointments, lunches, family errands, and professional projects not directly associated with the law firm, like podcast interviews and book editing. Having a four-day workweek motivates me to give 100 percent during those four days. Weekends are for leisure time with my family. This is what flexibility looks like. This is what work-life balance looks like. It doesn't need to involve typing a legal brief while breastfeeding or staying up until two in the morning to finish a project. It means looking at your life holistically, determining how you want and need to spend your time, and putting the puzzle pieces together in a way that feels right to you.

RUNNING YOUR CALENDAR LIKE A BOSS

Self-employment requires discipline. You don't need to work nine to five, but you do need to have a structured work schedule. I encouraged you to think about your ideal work day to meet your needs. If you have school-aged children and plan to work strictly during school hours, set your hours to nine to three and stick to them. If you have young kids in daycare but want to get an hour of exercise in right after drop-off, make your office hours ten to four. You may feel anxiety that other people won't understand or respect your schedule. It's your responsibility to set your own boundaries, and you don't need to explain your schedule beyond stating when you are and are not available. Decide the schedule you need. Decide when you are going to be available for consultations, phone calls, meetings, hearings, and legal work. In the early days of your firm, you may be doing it all. As you scale your firm and hire team members, your role and daily tasks may change, but I recommend that you still keep a regular schedule.

I find schedule blocking to be effective. This means you list out your primary tasks and assign them to specific time blocks throughout your week. A block schedule may look something like this:

5-DAY PLANNER

	MON	TUE	WED	THU	FRI
5:00am	Gym				
6:00am	Get ready				
7:00am	Get kids ready, pack lunches, school drop-off				
8:00am					
9:00am	Staff meeting				
10:00am	Staff meeting				
11:00am	Accounting meeting with bookkeeper				
12:00pm	Lunch meeting				
1:00pm	New client consultations				
2:00pm	New client consultations				
3:00pm	School pickup, activities				
4:00pm	School pickup, activities				
5:00pm	At home				
6:00pm	Dinner				
7:00pm	Bath & story time, put kids to bed				
8:00pm	Relax & read				
9:00pm	Sleep				
10:00pm	Sleep				
11:00pm	Sleep				
12:00am	Sleep				
1:00am	Sleep				
2:00am	Sleep				
3:00am	Sleep				
4:00am	Sleep				

Law can be such a rat race, with lawyers wearing their busyness as a badge of honor. Just check out of *all* of that. Set your work hours, and when scheduling things, adhere to your work hours. Your boundaries are important. You have other responsibilities to yourself and your family, and you don't need to compromise them for the convenience of others. Be reasonably accommodating, and respect your own calendar.

As you block out your schedule and determine how much time to set aside for certain kinds of work, here are some things to keep in mind.

CONSULTATIONS

As a brand new law firm owner, consultations take priority on your calendar. You want as many consultations and as much new business as possible coming in the door so you can grow your revenue and hire support staff. I want you to keep your schedule as open as possible for consultations, at least in the beginning. If that is overwhelming, offer consultations at least three or four days per week in the beginning.

You will get requests for consultations outside of your hours. For whatever reason, some people assume that lawyers take meetings at eight at night or on Sunday mornings. *We are not those lawyers.* Those lawyers are the ones who spend most of their time fantasizing about quitting their jobs. We are the lawyers running professional practices while maintaining healthy boundaries for our personal and family lives. We balance our time so we can show up for our clients and show up for our families, and have some time to ourselves. You want to be accessible for potential clients, but you don't need to be available on demand.

CLIENT COMMUNICATION

As with consultations, you want to be accessible to clients. However, you do not need to be readily available 24/7. I have never called a doctor's office and been transferred directly to the doctor. Most businesses don't have someone available to answer questions all night. If you have a virtual receptionist or answering service taking calls, set aside a specific time each day to respond to client calls and emails. Regardless of what type of law you practice, you are unlikely to regularly receive true emergency calls. Important does not automatically mean urgent. You can provide excellent client service and maintain reasonable boundaries.

At my firm, we have a client care coordinator whose job it is to take client calls and respond to messages and emails. We guarantee that calls and emails will be acknowledged within one business day. By acknowledged, I mean that we either respond to the client with an answer, or we let them know we received their message and are working on getting a substantive answer to them soon.

Do not use your personal cell phone for work calls. Do not have all calls go directly to you. I really want you to invest in a virtual answering service as early as possible, but if you absolutely cannot afford that at first, have calls go to a designated professional voicemail and spend the last hour of your workday returning messages. There is no way to be productive on all of your other tasks if you are taking direct calls all day. Dedicate a specific time each day to acknowledge or respond to clients. A same-day or one-day response time is perfectly acceptable, and allocating a specific time will minimize disruptions to the rest of your day. I also suggest making phone call appointments whenever possible. At my firm, phone calls with attorneys are scheduled the same way in-person meetings are. This avoids constant interruption and phone tag and is a more efficient way to handle communication. When you begin hiring support roles, you will take fewer calls because most questions will be answered by someone else. But even in the early days, if it is just you, develop a controlled and organized approach to communication.

MEETINGS AND HEARINGS

This is one area where you need to be prepared to assert yourself if needed. You are setting your own schedule and boundaries, but we work in a field where being a stressed out, over-scheduled workaholic is a point of pride for some of our colleagues. As with consultations, you need to have enough time in your schedule for meetings and hearings so that you can be reasonably flexible in scheduling with other people. However, you can still set boundaries. One of our goals is to normalize a work environment where even lawyers have personal lives that implicate whether we are available for work commitments.

Here is your script. For the purpose of this example, let's say your work hours are Monday through Thursday, nine to three. You drop off your kids at eight thirty a.m. and pick them up at three thirty.

Scenario 1: You are co-counseling a case with another lawyer and need to schedule a Zoom meeting to discuss assignments.

Co-Counsel: "I'm free after six this evening; does that work for you?"

You: "I can't do this evening, but I'm pretty flexible tomorrow morning or Wednesday around lunchtime. Let me know which of those times would work best for you."

Scenario 2: You are in court scheduling your next hearing in a case.

Judge: "The clerk tells me that the next available date is May 1 at eight thirty in the morning."

Opposing Counsel: "I'm available."

You: "I have a conflict at that time of day. Is there any room on the docket at ten in the morning, Your Honor?"

Scenario 3: A referring attorney wants to schedule a meeting with the potential client.

Referring Attorney: "We have the client scheduled for four tomorrow afternoon. Can you be here?"

You: "That's not a good time for me. Can we move it up to two? If not, I am wide open on Thursday and can be there any time between nine and three."

Scenario 4: You are handling a case with another lawyer and there is a filing deadline on Monday. It's Wednesday.

Referring Attorney: "I've been slammed all week, but I'll be in the office all day Saturday. I'll give you a call then, and we can put together a draft."

You: "Actually, I'm going to be out of pocket all weekend. I'll write a rough draft and send it over to you by the end of the day tomorrow. Then you can revise and do the final draft over the weekend. I'll be back in the office on Monday morning if we need to discuss anything before we file."

In each of these scenarios, you are being reasonable and accommodating while still adhering to your own boundaries. You generally don't need to explain why you aren't available at a date or time, and it's very unlikely that someone will ask. If they do, there is absolutely no shame in saying that you have childcare responsibilities and your work hours are X to Y. We should be normalizing the fact that working parents have parenting responsibilities, and that our jobs don't exist in a vacuum.

I'm not advising you to do anything I don't do myself. The scripts above are exactly how I regularly handle these situations. The *only* exceptions I make to my schedule *ever* are conferences or seminars I want to attend, a special professional event (like an evening holiday party), or when a case goes to trial. Those situations are infrequent and do not interfere with my responsibilities to my family. They are also scheduled well ahead of time, so I can easily make arrangements with my husband, another family member, or a sitter.

If your practice takes you to court regularly, you may be anxious about asserting scheduling boundaries there. For years, I was in court five days a week. I understand that there may be pressure to agree to certain dates or times. However, if you are being accommodating and available on multiple dates and times, you should expect professional courtesy in return. As I said, trials are an exception because they are all-day or multi-day events and involve several different parties. I'm talking about the standard motions hearings and status hearings where you can reasonably stay within your schedule.

Let me share an anecdote that had a huge impact on me. Years ago, I was in court scheduling a hearing with multiple attorneys. The clerk suggested a date in August. One of the lawyers said, "I'm not available at all in August." That was it, no long explanation, just a statement of her unavailability. The clerk moved on and we scheduled a hearing for September. Later, when we were in the lobby, she explained that every year she took the entire month of August off to go sailing. She had been doing this for years and she looked forward to it all year. She did not schedule anything for the month of August, period.

If you have a court-based practice currently, you may be thinking that there is simply no way you can maintain scheduling boundaries. I challenge you to examine whether you are overstating the difficulty of scheduling court as outlined above. However, if you truly cannot maintain your current practice area within your desired calendar, there are a few ways to handle this by referring back to Chapter One and considering your vision for your practice and your ideal case type. One solution would be to adjust your practice area, add additional case types that are not as court-intensive, and develop a niche that provides more flexibility. For example, if you are a criminal defense attorney in court five days a week, limit your trial work to more serious case types (lower volume and higher fee) and start handling more appeals, which involve mostly research and writing and require fewer court appearances. If you are a family lawyer handling frequent custody hearings, start building a niche in drafting prenuptial agreements for high net-worth clients. If you're an immigration lawyer, transition out of deportation defense (and lots of hearings) and focus on an administrative case type like employment visas or naturalization applications. Another solution is to set a short-term goal of hiring associate attorneys or contract attorneys to handle some or all of your court appearances.

Lawyers in a litigation-heavy practice can still have balanced schedules through delegation and teamwork. If your practice takes you to court frequently, prioritize adding associate attorneys to share the workload.

LEGAL WORK

If you have been practicing law at a firm or agency, this may be the role with which you are most familiar. When you begin your law practice, you will likely still be doing the bulk of the legal work. This will change and reduce over time, as you scale your firm and hire law clerks, paralegals, and associate attorneys. In fact, if your goal is to grow your practice, you should be actively reducing the amount of time you spend on legal work as soon as possible. For now, block off specific times during the week to do legal work. Consider hiring contract attorneys to help with time-intensive research and writing projects. There are companies like LawClerk that make it very easy to find quality contract attorneys.

Legal work is not as pressing as consultations or follow-up communication, so two blocks per week may be sufficient for you to research, write, or draft. There is always administrative work associated with legal work. If you have a virtual assistant, I recommend having one meeting with them to assign tasks for the week. If you are starting without any support staff, schedule a specific time to do administrative work, such as reviewing and scanning mail, taking checks to the bank, or putting together packages for filing. Be organized and intentional about your schedule, and don't just run around randomly putting out fires. The quality of your work will be much higher if you are spending a specific amount of dedicated time focused on each aspect of your practice rather than multitasking.

MARKETING

When creating a block schedule, do not forget about marketing. I'll discuss marketing in more detail in a later chapter; for now, know that you need to regularly spend time on creating and posting content, writing your newsletter, filming videos, and asking clients for reviews. Set aside one or two designated blocks throughout the week to create a plan for what you will be working on, write and film content, and respond to comments, reviews and messages across all of your social media platforms. I once heard someone say marketing is not a faucet you turn on when you want more business—it needs to be a slow and steady stream of content to build consistent revenue.

NETWORKING

I suggest setting specific goals for networking, like committing to attending one event per month. Because there are so many virtual networking opportunities, it is easier than ever to fit networking into your schedule. If you're in a Facebook group where you're likely to find potential clients or referral partners, commit to posting once a week. If you're in multiple groups or platforms, set aside thirty minutes to scan posts and see if there is anything relevant. Cultivate your existing network and leave some room to expand it. For example, leave one time slot per month open for coffee or lunch with a colleague. These meetings don't need to be for a particular *reason*; they're to help you remain engaged in your community and nurture relationships.

PERSONAL/PROFESSIONAL DEVELOPMENT

This may be something you schedule outside of your business hours, but it is important nonetheless. If you have a fifteen-minute commute each way, you can listen to a podcast episode in the car. Read a business book each month, setting aside some time in the early morning or before bed. If you often have downtime, like waiting in court or taking a train ride, slip your e-reader into your bag. Prioritize learning and growing in business. I have several law- and business-related podcasts I listen to weekly, and I attend several law firm management conferences each year.

FAMILY/HOME TIME

You've been pining for balance, so make sure there is time in your day where you feel like you can show up for your family guilt-free. The ideal balance will change over time based on your individual needs. We have three school-aged children at home, and two are very young. When I leave the office around two thirty, I am done with work. I pick them up at three and spend the afternoons with them until my husband gets home from work around six, and then we start dinner. We go swimming, get ice cream and go to the park, or do a craft project. Sometimes, we just go home and have a snack and hang around. They tell me about their day and show me their artwork. Sometimes, I just sit on the patio and read a magazine while they play. When everyone is home, my husband typically cooks dinner and then cleans up while I do the bath time/pajamas/story routine, which is something I love. This time is important to me, and our afternoons together provide constant affirmation of the life I chose. My kids know that I work, and they know my work is an important part of my day. I also want them to see me having fun, feeling relaxed, and enjoying time with them.

I'm not the first working mom to discover this balance. In fact, none other than Justice Ruth Bader Ginsburg approached work-life balance this way when her children were young and she was fighting her way through Harvard Law School. "I went to class about 8:30 a.m., and I came home at 4 p.m.; that was children's hour. It was a total break in my day, and children's hour continued until Jane went to sleep," she said in a 2017 interview. "I felt each part of my life gave me respite from the other."[14] Future US Supreme Court Justice, trailblazing pioneer, and the OG of lawyer moms spent the afternoons with her children when they were young. The rest of the story goes that she stayed up all night studying...but I'm not trying to get on the Supreme Court. The takeaway is that our work life and our home life, specifically time with kids, can complement one another and make us better in both roles.

SELF-CARE

In creating a balanced schedule, don't forget about yourself. You made the leap into entrepreneurship to, at least in part, have a healthier and balanced life *for yourself*. No matter how you do it, balancing law and business and motherhood takes a lot of energy. You need to be refilling your own cup, as well. Now that you set your schedule, allocate time when you don't need to answer to anyone else. Time when you can turn off your phone and email, and the kids are at school or daycare. You don't need to answer legal questions, or direct an employee, or get anyone a snack. Maybe this is an hour a day, or maybe it's a time block per week. I take a few hours on Fridays to exercise, run personal errands, get my nails done, or have a lunch date with my husband. This time does not interfere with my other responsibilities, and it helps me stay sane. You owe it to yourself to stay healthy—physically and mentally—so that you can show up in your roles at work and at home. Remember, for years men have been disappearing for eight hours at a time to play golf and passing it off as a legitimate work obligation. Go on a weekly hike or get a monthly massage, or make a standing coffee date with a friend. You deserve to be happy and healthy. This is not just a luxury. It will directly improve your performance at work and your sanity at home.

Now that you have visualized your ideal schedule and law practice, it is time to develop the professional image for your firm. Your branding is going to influence how you market yourself, how you run your firm, and how you interact with your future clients.

CHAPTER 5

DETERMINING YOUR IMAGE

Looks matter. I want you to abandon any version of "my clients won't care" or "my work speaks for itself." Yes, they do; and no, it won't. Being a good lawyer should be a given, and is a minimum threshold requirement for running a successful law firm. I'm going to expect and assume that you provide excellent legal representation to clients. This book is not about being a lawyer—that's what we all went to law school for. This book is about how to build a business, one where we attract and maintain clients and make money.

You should put some thought into the image you want your firm to convey to potential clients and colleagues. Developing an image that is consistent with your vision of the firm will lend itself to your branding, as well as maintaining a cohesive identity as you add team members and scale the business.

LOGO AND BRANDING

Once you select the name of your business, put some thought

into branding. I'm not telling you to spend thousands of dollars on a branding package before you open your doors. Branding is something that can be changed and upgraded over time as your business grows and evolves. I evolved my firm from a partnership (which changed names twice in the first three years) to my current entity as a single-member S corporation; and I've changed my name, logo and branding along the way. If you are planning to launch your firm, have some fun thinking about the look.

Branding in the beginning is fun, and it's a good exercise to think about how you want to present yourself to the world. I think of branding as establishing the vibe of your law firm. What image or feeling do you want to present? These feelings can be portrayed through color, symbolism, and language. A logo, slogan, or color scheme can help set you apart beyond the typical scales of justice imagery popular in law. Go back to your original vision—who are you serving, and what case types will you handle? A firm specializing in adoption may want soft colors and parent/child imagery. A firm serving international business clients might opt for globe or map imagery.

My firm is women-led, and our vibe gives off confidence, reassurance, and compassion to clients who are facing a crisis. My favorite color is teal, and all of our branding uses a particular shade of teal (our designer actually created it and named it "Airington Teal"—how cool is that?) and created a recognizable logo. We use this in our marketing, office materials, and client gifts for consistency. This branding is consistent throughout our advertising and even our office decor. Being a mother is part of my personal image, and we regularly reference this in our marketing. Motherhood conveys to clients compassion, trustworthiness, and protectiveness.

There are a lot of low-cost options for creating a logo if, like me, you have absolutely no artistic sense. Some marketing companies will include logo creation in a package (more on marketing later). If you are not starting with a marketing package or website design that includes logo development, you can use a freelance artist on a site like Fiverr to develop a logo. You can literally get a logo designed for under $100. Again, there is no need to overthink this or spend much money on it up front. But come up with at least a starting point and feel free to evolve as you grow. Thinking about your vision and firm identity is important, and if you're ready and have the money, branding your very own business is a ton of fun.

DESIGN YOUR OFFICE

Running a law firm is running a business, and any business should care how it presents itself to potential clients. How do you want your office to look? How do you want clients to feel when they walk in the door? The design of your office is one of the first impressions you make. Don't limit yourself to what a law firm is supposed to look like. Brown leather and lady justice memorabilia? That's fine if it's what you want.

I'm just going to say it: my office is beautiful. I love walking into it in the morning. My team has a nice place to work. Nearly everyone who walks in the door comments on how lovely the office is.

My office actually looks a lot like my house—contemporary, natural wood, my favorite color (teal), soft furniture, modern artwork on the walls... Be intentional and put some thought into it. If you can afford to consult or even shop through an interior designer, I highly recommend it. I don't have an eye for design, so it's worthwhile for me to have help in my office and my home. However, that's not always an option in the beginning. For my first office, it was definitely *not* in the budget. I bought a used desk set from a mid-century modern used furniture store (I love it, and I still have the desk). When I scaled up to my first full office suite, I made a fairly significant investment and worked with an interior designer and bought quality furniture. When I scaled a second time into my current office, I kept all of the same furniture and decor and supplemented it with some additional coordinating pieces to fill the larger space. Although spending so much money on office furniture and decor scared me at the time, now—five years later—I am convinced it was an excellent investment (and all of the original furniture still looks brand new). The designer helped me choose rugs and fabric for the reception furniture that were meant to take abuse and are easy to clean. Yes, I have had a white couch in my reception area for five years, and it still looks brand new. When I moved into a bigger office, I kept the style consistent and added on to what we had.

The reason why I advocate for investing in your office appearance is three-fold. One, it really does have an impact on prospective clients. When new or prospective clients walk into an office that looks and feels upscale, it sends a message that this is a success-ful law firm. That inspires confidence and comfort. If you had a legal issue and needed to consult with a lawyer, imagine two scenarios: 1) you walk into an immaculate, modern office and sip coffee on a comfortable couch while you wait; or 2) you walk into a dingy, cramped office and sit on a cracked leather couch (or stained office chair) while you wait. Which feels better? Which inspires confidence? Furthermore, where will you feel more comfortable spending a significant amount of money for professional guidance?

And please don't buy into the narrative that if your office looks too nice it will deter clients because they'll think you are too expensive. Just don't. Don't play small—not with your office, and not with yourself. Have you ever walked into a business and thought, "Wow, this is way too pleasant?" No. You're going to be big-time. You deserve a nice office, and your clients deserve to walk into a nice environment.

Two, investing in your office has an impact on office morale. If you don't already have staff, you will soon. Where do you think people would prefer to work? A bright, clean office with coordinated decor and new or quality furniture? Yep.

Three, it has an impact on *you*. When I walk into my office in the morning, I feel proud of the space. Our reception area is pretty and inviting. Everyone on my team looks comfortable in their workspace. My office makes me feel like a boss. Later on, I will share some tips on getting ready to open your doors. But as a foundation, you need a fresh, clean, and comfortable office to serve as the canvas for the amazing work you are going to do.

Seriously consider my plea to stay away from the typical icky office furniture. We can do better than orange veneer wood and vinyl seats in faded geometric prints. We can do better than hand-me-down wingback chairs. Do not put metal filing cabinets in your office—you are not a probation officer. Get some style. Put down an area rug and hang artwork on the walls. No, your law school diploma isn't artwork. People are going to know you're a lawyer because you have a law firm. Let's normalize not decorating a space with crappy diploma frames. Do you want a traditional look? A modern look? Pick an actual style, create a Pinterest board (if that's your thing), and put some thought into your office. You'll be spending time there, other people will be working there, and it will be a significant part of the first impression you make on clients.

Don't be intimidated and feel like you need to spend five figures on furniture to open your doors. You absolutely do not. As I said, I made that investment several years into my practice, after working just fine from my secondhand desk. However, I do think it is critical to make your office attractive, which is totally possible on a budget. Pinterest can be your friend to help you find a look you like. Buy online, or even on CraigsList, if you can find what you want. Whatever your starting budget is, find a way to put your best face forward to prospective clients. Maybe that means focusing on a nice reception area and using a hand-me-down desk in your private office.

As you design your office, don't just think about the decor, but also think about the layout. My office is on the first floor of a modern building atrium. When you enter our suite, you walk into a bright, beautifully decorated reception area with comfortable seating and a coffee station. We have a modern reception desk and a large, attractive sign. Right off of reception is our conference room, with contemporary furniture and artwork. I chose the setup specifically to have a "front of house" area which avoids clients needing to ever come to the "back of house." This design maintains a calm and quiet environment for prospective client meetings, and it protects client confidentiality while staff are on the phone with the court or discussing client matters. It maintains a quiet, relaxing space for clients to wait and meet with an attorney rather than hearing phones ringing and printers buzzing. The separation maintains the image I want to portray to clients, and it makes both clients and my team feel comfortable. If you have a "front of house," prioritize furniture and decor for the part of your office that clients will see. Some buildings have shared amenities, like a conference room, which means one less room for you to furnish.

LOOK THE PART

Do you look the part? Remember how I said looks matter when it comes to office environment? Well, looks matter for us, too. I want you to dress professionally all the time, regardless of whether you have staff or you're alone in your office, and whether you see clients in person or not. From now on, you are part of your brand. The way you present yourself to clients sets the tone for your relationship with them. The way you dress and behave will set the tone for your future team as your firm grows. If you think this is too basic or condescending, it's not, because there are lawyers who go to work in yoga pants. Don't be one of those lawyers.

Edith Head, renowned Hollywood costume designer, once said, "You can have anything you want in life if you dress for it." Ever heard the phrase "dress for success?" In 2014, Yale School of Management actually published a study on this. The study included two groups of people engaged in a business exercise. One group dressed professionally, and the other dressed more casually. The professionally-dressed ones performed better in the study, taking leadership roles, displaying greater confidence, and making a significantly higher profit. The takeaway is that not only does how we dress impact how others perceive us, but it also actually impacts how we see ourselves (and how we behave). I "dress" for work every day, whether I have meetings scheduled or not. My entire team does, as well. Anyone could stop in at our office unexpectedly and find a team of people who look like they know what they're doing.

I know 2020 became the year of working in your pajama pants, but let's put them back in bed where they belong. Draw a line in the sand and say, "I am never going to wear athleisure or flip-flops to work. I am never going to wear a struggle bun to work." I'm not saying you need to adhere to a strict business formal dress code. I do not wear pantyhose, period. I rarely wear suits. They're uncomfortable and don't flatter my body. If you already have a style you like, keep it. If you left a work environment with a dress code you hated, now is your chance to update it.

When I first opened a practice, I discovered a company called M.M. LaFleur. I basically bought a few of their dresses and wore them almost exclusively for several years. They are classic, stretchy, and pretty perfect for work, including court or travel. Stretchy dresses were important because a) they were super comfortable, and b) remember how I had a baby basically the same day I started my practice? If you are experimenting with a new style, or if shopping stresses you out, or it's just not your thing, I suggest this route. Many of M.M. LaFleur's dresses are machine-washable, and they also come in extended sizes. This company is made for working moms and especially lawyers. As I transitioned out of regular court appearances and into a more executive role at my firm, I expanded my look to include outfits appropriate for meetings, if not ideal for court.

In sum, no excuses. You can be comfortable and look professional. The pandemic did not "change workwear forever" in a way that involves pajamas. No one wants to place their confidence in—and hand over tons of money to—a lawyer wearing yoga pants. You can express personal style and look professional, too. You are a business owner now, and I want you to look good no matter what the day brings. Every single interaction can be a chance to expand your business. You might have a potential client walk in without an appointment. You might run into a fellow tenant in the elevator who can refer business. You might see another lawyer you know at Target and mention you've opened a practice. I was recently hired at the nail salon by someone who overheard me talking to the nail technician. Never, ever be caught in a potential business opportunity in sweat pants and a messy bun. Leave your house (or get on Zoom) looking like the absolute badass you are.

Now you and your office are ready to start serving clients. So, where will your clients come from? If you are already in private practice, you may have a book of business you are bringing with you. If you are leaving the public sector, or you are reentering the workforce after a break, you may be starting from scratch. No worries. Your future clients are out there—you just need to let them know how to find you.

CHAPTER 6

FINDING NEW CLIENTS

Marketing is one of the areas that intimidate new firm owners the most. Historically, the legal field has made it very difficult or even taboo to market. For many years, lawyers were not even permitted to advertise. It was generally accepted that if a lawyer was any good, then word would spread among clientele, and eventually they would have a flourishing practice. In 1977, the US Supreme Court heard an appeal from two Arizona attorneys who were sanctioned by their state bar for advertising their law firm in a newspaper. The Supreme Court held that legal advertising was protected speech and that the state bar's restrictions on legal advertising violated the First Amendment.[15]

Although legal advertising has been protected for over forty years, it is still taboo in some circles, particularly among senior lawyers. Some practice areas adapted more easily to advertising than others. Personal injury, bankruptcy and medical malpractice lawyers seem to have adopted advertising early. Other practice areas are a little late to the game. In conversations with other lawyers, I find that many have an overly conservative approach to marketing. If you have any preconceived ideas or stigmas toward legal marketing, please abandon them. The traditional idea of building a great reputation and having that develop into a bustling practice is not mutually exclusive to marketing your services. You can be a great lawyer with an awesome reputation *and* use marketing to let even more people know about it. The idea of building a successful business without any marketing is ridiculous. There is no reason to rely on word of mouth alone, or to wait years or decades to let your practice build up naturally.

You should actively work to get your name out there. Building a great local reputation should be a given. Many of our firm clients are referred from past clients, local colleagues, and acquaintances. I am proud of the firm's local reputation. We use marketing to amplify that reputation, broaden our reach, and add value to our consumers and followers.

FIRST THINGS FIRST: KNOW THE RULES

There are still professional regulations regarding advertising. Read the rules of conduct in your state to understand any specifics. If you have a particular concern, some state bars have a process where you can submit an advertisement for review.

In general, the idea is that we do not want to be misleading, make false promises, or harass people with unsolicited offers. Make sure you are protecting client confidentiality, or you have client consent to share anything identifiable. Understand when you are required to label something as advertising, and also where you are required to include disclaimers.

DIGITAL PRESENCE: WEBSITE

You need a website. It's 2022. Companies have had websites for almost thirty years. We don't need to talk about this much beyond my saying that no legitimate business should be without a great website. We can't even entertain that. Please don't rely on online lawyer directories. Please don't have your teenage nephew build you a website. Please don't use your personal Facebook page as your business site.

You do not need to spend a fortune on your first website, but you need to have one, and it needs to look good. Why? Everyone looks everything up online. No matter your primary source of business—past clients, referrals from colleagues, traditional advertising—people will look you up online. Literally the first thing I do when someone recommends any company, product, or service is Google it. If a friend told me they knew the best lawyer in the universe for my issue and gave me their personal number, I would *still* look them up online. What do you want people to see when they Google your name?

There are countless companies that build websites. If you are going to work with a marketing company, they may build your website as part of their offer. I have had several websites over the years. Currently, I work with a legal marketing company called Scorpion. They built my website, and they run it from their platform because it's all interconnected to the ads they run and the monthly marketing metrics they monitor for me.

If you're not ready for a marketing package, that's perfectly fine. Purchase your domain name (mine is www.airingtonlaw. com) from a host. There are many companies who are hosts, like Domain.com, GoDaddy, and HostGator. Once you own a domain name, you can create new websites down the road with the same website address. Look at other law firms whose websites you admire, and ask who created their site. Schedule consultations with a few web design and marketing companies to see what they have to offer. If you are not tech savvy, keep in mind that not all websites are created equal. You want to work with someone who understands legal marketing and can walk you through concepts like search engine optimization and the pros and cons of certain types of content. There are various ways a professional can optimize your website, increase your online visibility, and even track metrics that you can later use to inform other marketing decisions.

At an absolute minimum, you need a nice-looking landing page that people will find when they search for you or your firm. Beyond that, your website is an opportunity to impress potential clients. For many prospective clients, your website will be their first real impression of your firm. While you don't need the perfect website the moment you open your doors, there is really no reason not to have a good one in light of how many affordable options exist for website design.

SOCIAL MEDIA

Think you're too cool for social media? Are you someone (like my husband) who considers it a point of pride to be able to say you're "not on social media?" Think again, because you're about to be on social media. Social media is no longer cutting-edge marketing. Like having a website, it is an absolute non-negotiable in my opinion. I don't care if you use it personally. As of July 2022, there were 4.7 *billion* social media users worldwide.[16] This is about 60 percent of the world's population.

Not only is social media the vehicle through which you can reach most of the world's population, but it is a place for free advertising. There is the option for paid advertising, but it is free to have an account and publish content.

Social media may be silly, or frivolous, or evil, depending on your point of view. That's fine. You don't need to hang out there. You don't even need to go on at all, if you choose (and can afford) to have a company or person moderate your firm's presence for you. But you do need to have your business up there—for the exposure, legitimacy, and accessibility to the majority of the planet's inhabitants, which surely includes your prospective clients. Digital marketing—and social media, in particular—is an incredible marketing option for a fledgling business because you can reach thousands (millions…billions?) of people for free. Even paid advertising on social media is extremely low-cost compared to traditional print, radio, or television advertising; and it has the potential to reach a much larger audience.

Use social media to introduce yourself as a lawyer and as a practice. Share information about the type of work you do and how you do it. Your social media should still be professional, but it is a way to personalize your marketing. Photos and videos of you will help potential clients feel like they know you. Informational posts help establish that you know what you're doing. Social media is also a network, where you can build mutual followings with not only potential clients, but also referral sources. You need to plan to post regularly, either personally or outsourced to a social media manager or marketing service. You want to build up your available content, which raises your profile online. When people come across your pages, you want them to see recent, valuable content and a professional look. Just as people will Google you, they will also search for your firm on social media. Be there and look good.

Create your social media pages as soon as you have your name. That way, you can start putting some content up and pick up some followers. Send out "requests to like" to everyone on your personal contact list. Don't be shy; everyone does it, and it's not a big deal. It lets people in your near and far circles know that you are opening a firm. If someone doesn't want to follow you, they can ignore or unfollow you. Announce your opening date and location or post a video talking about how excited you are to open your firm, and what kinds of cases you will be doing. Don't overthink it—just get content out there. If you scroll back years on my firm's social media, you'll see my content and style have changed drastically. Follow other lawyers and law firms to see what's out there and get ideas for content or style. As with the website, there's no reason not to have your social media set up by Day One.

Some ideas for posting content:

- an introductory "About Me" post (photo with text, or video)
- an introduction of your staff
- a virtual tour of your office
- photos from around your city, outside the courthouse, or working at a local coffee shop (make sure you check in or tag the locations)
- case types you handle
- legal tip of the day
- weird law facts (apparently it's illegal to flip a coin to decide who pays for coffee in Richmond, Virginia—who knew?)
- your two cents on a high-profile case getting media coverage
- an announcement of a case win
- a selfie with a client after a favorable outcome (with client consent)
- an announcement of an award won by you or someone in your firm
- "know your rights" videos (with disclaimer that it is for informational purposes, not legal advice)
- a myth or fact about your practice area ("possession is nine-tenths of the law" is not actually a defense to a theft charge)

When thinking about what to post, look for ways to add value with helpful, interesting, or entertaining information. You want people to be interested in your content and follow you and become familiar with your firm. The idea is not that people hop on Instagram and search for a lawyer when they need one. Rather, the point is to gain a following, raise your profile, and become a familiar face and name in your field, so that when someone does need a lawyer, you are at the top of their mind.

Social media is constantly evolving, and it's important to stay up to date on new apps and monitor how other lawyers are using them. Different platforms have different target audiences and styles. You can develop your own style, and approach the different platforms in different ways. Think about which apps your ideal clients are on—but keep in mind that these trends are shifting, and you may have ideal clients across multiple platforms. Don't be intimidated by a platform or feel like you need to have professional-grade content immediately. Just get started and get some content up there. At a minimum, I recommend getting your firm on Facebook and Instagram. Understand that waiting may put you behind the curve on other platforms. You will evolve your pages over time, and as you scale, you will likely engage professional help at some point.

For social media legal marketing beginners, here is my layperson summary of the different platforms and where you want to be seen and why. The following platforms are the most popular, and in my experience, marketing on their apps can be very successful.

FACEBOOK

Facebook is still the most-used social media platform on Earth. As of January 2022, there were 2.912 billion users worldwide. About 70 percent of Americans report using Facebook. It remains popular among various age groups, and it is almost equally balanced in terms of political identity among users.[17] Most people are there, and you should be there, too—for free. While you can pay to boost posts or run ads on Facebook, there is no cost to having a business page and posting regular content. Post short videos announcing case wins or introducing you and your team members. Share photos of your new office and link to any news coverage of your cases. If you share or link an article, make sure you include a comment connecting it back to your practice. Keep the language and content engaging—no lengthy legal analyses.

INSTAGRAM

About 40 percent of Americans use Instagram.[18] Its users are evenly split between men and women, and it is most common among eighteen-to-thirty-four-year- olds. Instagram is designed to share photo and video content, and while users can like and comment, it tends not to spark the same kind of lengthier interactions as Facebook.

Instagram is easy to use, and you can introduce yourself to potential clients visually by sharing videos of your office, your team, or even your city. Our firm may share photos from outside the courthouse after a win, photos of a team member handing a client their green card, or a short video announcement about the firm. You can share something in a permanent post or in a temporary story. Short videos can be posts or stories, and longer videos can be added as reels. Instagram has a function to automatically share to Facebook, so you can link your firm accounts and post to both simultaneously from Instagram.

YOUTUBE

Eighty-one percent of Americans use YouTube.[19] You can create a YouTube channel for free and post video content to it. Upload videos of you introducing yourself, talking about your firm, or explaining legal issues. YouTube videos can be longer and more educational than videos on other platforms. Unlike Facebook or Instagram, where people are going to be scrolling and watching short clips, users may sit and watch a longer video on YouTube if it is interesting.

A good way to use YouTube is to create educational videos about the type of law you practice. What are some FAQs or myths about your practice area? What are some things you wish people knew about your practice area? If you are a criminal lawyer, film a "know your rights" video series. If you are a wills and estates lawyer, do a video series on estate planning need-to-knows. If you are a personal injury lawyer, tell viewers what they should do in case of an accident. Through this type of video, you are a) giving viewers value through information; b) showing that you are an expert in your field; and c) naturally increasing your profile. These are all aspects of marketing, but it feels natural as you share information and educate consumers.

LINKEDIN

About 28 percent of Americans use LinkedIn.[20] LinkedIn is a professional network, and while many use the platform to hire or look for jobs, it's another opportunity to have a professional profile. I find LinkedIn to be lower maintenance than the other platforms because users tend to post less content and things don't move as quickly.

Because your professional network is going to be an important referral source, you want your profile to be updated and make clear what type of work you are doing. I once received a referral from an attorney I had known for over ten years. He told me he had no idea I handled that particular case type until he happened to see a post about it on our firm's LinkedIn page. That is a great example of where personal networking and social media marketing go hand in hand. He already knew me and had a generally good opinion of me, but he didn't know I'd be a good fit for that case type until he saw it on LinkedIn.

If you don't already have a personal profile, create one. Then, create a business profile for your page. Include all of your updated information. Spend half an hour sending out as many connection invitations as you can think of, and then write a post announcing your new firm.

TWITTER

About 22 percent of Americans use Twitter, and users tend to be younger with higher education and income levels.[21] Twitter is very fast-moving and often circles around trending news stories. Users can tweet their own commentary or re-tweet or share another person's tweet. In my personal experience, a Twitter feed is not integral to law firm marketing. If you are partial to the platform, or if your practice area often intersects with hot news stories, then it probably makes sense for you to maintain a profile.

TIKTOK

About 21 percent of Americans use TikTok, including almost half of all eighteen-to-twenty-nine-year-olds and a quarter of thirty-to-forty-eight-year-olds.[22] In 2022, TikTok is still a new frontier for legal marketing, but plenty of lawyers were early adopters. It is decidedly more casual and creative than any other social media app. Content is video, and you can either record and edit a video and post it, or go live. Perhaps more so than other apps, there is a wide range of styles among lawyers on TikTok. This app is largely for entertainment, so cheeky content is going to be more popular than serious content. Some lawyers post short commentaries on trending legal cases, funny stories about being a lawyer, or interesting tidbits about the law. Different songs, soundbites, or dances can help users trend on TikTok. You can respond to messages or comments, or offer up a curated "ask me anything." As with all platforms, if you are using a profile for professional purposes, keep certain professional guidelines. Sharing your personality is effective, but avoid anything embarrassing, too controversial, or far removed from your practice.

GROWING YOUR SOCIAL MEDIA PRESENCE

Social media is a critical opportunity for your business, so we're not going to have your kids' babysitter running your Facebook account. We're not hiring a high school intern to run the key advertising platform for your law firm. Digital marketing is a professional field, and there are tons of affordable options to get professional assistance.

As you are starting out, I recommend focusing on the platform you think is most likely to engage your ideal client. Once you are comfortable using video and generating content, expand to other platforms. While you are DIY, use a program like Canva to make your posts look professional and consistent. Set yourself a schedule, such as posting to social media on Monday, Wednesday, and Friday. You can schedule posts in advance on several platforms, such as Facebook and Instagram. If you are concerned about remembering to post regularly, pick one day a week and set aside thirty minutes to write several posts, and schedule them to publish throughout the week. Challenge yourself to record at least one short video a week—for example, every Friday afternoon, post a short video announcing a good case result or sharing a legal tip. You can record a one-minute video sitting in your car at the school pickup line. If you're feeling self-conscious about how you look, pick a day when you feel confident and batch your videos—record several videos on that day and save them to post throughout the week.

When you're ready to delegate social media management to someone else, there are a million companies offering various services. Many companies will offer monthly plans based on the number of platforms and the number of posts. For example, a company may charge a monthly fee of $750 to post three times per week on two or three platforms. This may involve somewhat generic content. If you scroll through Instagram and look at law firm pages, many of them have very similar styles. That's not a bad way to start off, building up a professional-looking page and content, but make sure you are also posting some pictures and videos to personalize it.

As you build up your business and revenue, you can invest in a more personalized social media presence. For a more individualized approach, you may collaborate with a marketing company to plan out cohesive themes or campaigns, add professional photography, and get more creative with video. These days, mid-size and larger law firms often have marketing departments with in-house employees handling the firm's online presence.

For the first several years, I was heavily involved in my firm's social media presence. I posted updates, photos, and videos multiple times a week. Eventually, I hired an agency to handle posting some of my content to keep it constant and also to create a more professional look. As I grew, I moved on to a different agency giving more individualized attention to our content strategy. Today, I have a full-time team member who handles our marketing and community engagement, and we work with various vendors for video production, paid advertising, and search engine optimization. Even though we have different professionals working on our marketing, I still post photos and videos to our accounts to maintain engagement and add personalization.

VIDEO AND PHOTOGRAPHY

I cannot count how many lawyers have told me they want to do more on social media but are intimidated by making videos. We're talking about lawyers who do regular public speaking and take cases to trial. All you need for video is your phone. If you want to invest another $50, buy a basic ring light with a bluetooth remote control. A ring light will hold your phone toward you and shine light directly on you. This improves the quality of the video and gives you more options because you can create the video hands-free. Just start creating some videos and post them on your pages on the different platforms discussed. You can also broadcast live on several of these platforms, and those videos then save to your video library. Facebook, Instagram, and TikTok all have functions to help you easily go live. You can also use an application like Streamyard, which syncs with Facebook, to give your live video a more professional look by including your branding and contact information. Video personalizes your online presence and makes potential clients feel that they know and trust you even before meeting. For more on why video is important in legal marketing, and how to use it, I highly recommend *The Game Changing Attorney* by Michael Mogill.

Professional photos are fairly easy and affordable to do early on, while you're getting set up. Hire a local photographer to at least do a professional headshot. Often, they will offer packages to take a few different photos that you can use now or down the road on your website and social media. At a minimum, have a current professional headshot to put on the Internet. I update mine every few years, and our team photo needs to be updated every time we add more people. Having photographs online helps personalize your marketing and makes it easier for prospective clients to connect with you. You can also recycle different photos throughout your marketing, so having shots in different outfits and poses can be useful when creating ads and posts.

PAID ADVERTISING

I did not do any paid advertising for several years. Many lawyers I know report that Google ads is their primary method of marketing. I grew my digital presence with social media *first* before I committed to paid advertising. Neither way is wrong, but advertising can get very expensive and may be out of budget in the early days of a firm. My advice is to wait on paid advertising unless you are very well funded. This applies to both digital paid ads and traditional ads. You can generate a lot of business without it, and then scale up to paid advertising when you can fund it. Paid ads and promotions on Facebook and Instagram can be done easily and fairly inexpensively. Facebook will actually give you the option of promoting a post or turning it into an advertisement; you can set a small budget to try it out and see how it does. Google ads are more expensive, and a digital marketing company can help create an ad, set it up, and track its effectiveness.

Many law firms, including my own, also use traditional marketing methods. There are still newspaper and magazine ads, billboards, radio and television ads, and direct mail. Some forms of advertising lend themselves to particular practice areas. A billboard in a high-traffic area will probably be a better investment if you are a personal injury lawyer specializing in auto accidents than if you are an intellectual property lawyer specializing in trademark and copyright for artists. A radio ad on a local Spanish-language radio channel might make sense for an immigration lawyer serving Spanish-speaking clients. These traditional marketing options are significantly more expensive, and probably won't be one of the early investments you make into marketing. I suggest starting with what you can afford; but don't get lazy with marketing. You will want your business to continually grow, and I have found that the most effective strategy is to use multiple marketing methods at once. There is no single silver bullet. I encourage you to view growth through marketing as an evolving business investment.

NETWORKING

With all the bells and whistles of digital marketing, it's easy to forget about old-fashioned networking. One is not a substitute for the other. In fact, they complement each other. While I believe social media marketing is extremely important, I also know there is immense value in personal connection through networking. You can start networking for your business the moment you decide to start a firm. You don't need to have a name or an office and any other details nailed down. As a business owner (or soon-to-be-business owner) you need to start selling yourself and your services *yesterday*. Shout from the rooftops that you're opening a law firm. Post about it on your personal social media.

Networking within the legal community is pretty obvious. Local bar associations or specialty bar associations are great places to start. If you've been practicing in your area, you may already be a member of some of these organizations. If you're brand new to law or the area, go to a few events to see which organizations seem the most beneficial. Once you've identified two or three groups, try to go to events on a semi-regular basis. I've been a member of the women's bar association for years, and most of their events are weekday luncheons which make it easy to attend as a working mom. Being a regular at events will naturally result in important professional relationships. When you go to bar association events, don't just stand around. Just showing up doesn't really count. Get to know people and make sure people know what you do, and be specific. Don't assume that other lawyers in your practice area are direct competition. In conversation, work in mentions of what case types you are handling. Lawyers love telling war stories, so don't be shy about mentioning a cool case you've done in your practice area.

I get many referrals from other lawyers, both within my practice areas and from outside my own circle. As you're introducing yourself or socializing, mention the types of cases you work on. You want your colleagues to associate you with your ideal case types so that you can stay at the top of their minds for referrals; and, likewise, you want to have a short list of trusted colleagues to refer clients to for other matters. Set a goal to attend at least one event per month if you are new to the community, or at least one per quarter to maintain existing connections.

After an event, go home and connect via LinkedIn, Facebook, or Instagram with some of the people you met in person. Fellow lawyers will likely be important referral sources, and it is mutually beneficial to have strong professional relationships with colleagues. Keep a list of lawyers you want to refer cases to, as well. Once you open your doors, you will get some calls for case types you don't do (especially while you are still tweaking your marketing efforts). Rather than turn down a consultation, you can refer them to a colleague and follow up via email. If another attorney refers a client to you, call or email them to say thanks. If an attorney sends you multiple referrals, an occasional thank you gift may be appropriate. If you have questions about gifts for referral partners, check your state bar rules. In my state, a thank you gift is perfectly fine as long as it is not given as compensation to *solicit* future referrals. I periodically send flowers or drop off a bottle of wine for colleagues with whom I have regular or long-term relationships.

Do not limit your marketing to other lawyers. While local bar participation should be a given, there are networking opportunities well outside the legal community. You want everyone in your life to know that you are a lawyer, and what types of cases you handle. You can accomplish this in a way that is not annoying or overly aggressive. Social media makes it easy to connect with people and expose them to information indirectly. If you meet a bunch of fellow parents at a birthday party, friend or connect with or follow them on social media afterward. In other settings, use opportunities to introduce yourself subtly as a lawyer. I find that people just seem to remember when someone is a lawyer. It's an easily identifiable profession, versus "I don't know, I think so-and-so's dad does something with computers." This is important, because down the road when someone you have met—or someone they know—needs a lawyer, you will come to mind. Yes, you will get some calls outside of your practice area, but you will refer those out. You will also become a target for random legal questions, but that's an occupational hazard.

The goal is for you and your business to become very visible and well-known in your area. Your immediate circle of friends, neighbors, colleagues, and acquaintances is the starting point.

I have made professional connections at my children's schools, my husband's company, a local non-profit where I volunteer, my yoga studio, and an outdoor exercise group. Anyone is a potential client, referral source, or collaborator. Over ten years ago, while I was on a run with the workout group, I struck up a conversation with the woman next to me. I learned that she was a realtor, and it just so happened that a few days later I decided I wanted to buy a house. Since then, I have bought and sold three homes with her *and* referred several friends to her. That is networking—being out and about, participating in events, and getting to know people. Women often feel discomfort when promoting themselves, however, because we have been socialized to be modest and not show off. You are a business now, and tasteful self-promotion is important because you need people to know who you are and what type of work you do.

If you previously worked for a large corporation, firm, or government agency, your networking probably looked different than it will now as a law firm owner. Rather than focusing on your own professional network for individual opportunities, you are casting a wider net throughout your community. Combine a strong digital presence with on-the-ground relationship-building to solidify your position and raise the profile of your business.

COMMUNITY ENGAGEMENT

A small business should be engaged in the local community.

Our circle of influence is a critical starting point to building a network of clients; community engagement is a natural extension of your own circle. Community engagement can include sponsoring a local organization, attending events, volunteering, donating, hosting a legal clinic, or giving a presentation. These are all ways to simultaneously give value to the community and build your firm's profile. Our firm has done free legal talks through the local law school, various churches, and a few businesses. We have booths at festivals where we combine fun things like raffles and prizes with free mini-intakes. Some of this will be purely community service, and some may result directly in paying clients. Either way, the more you are out in the community, supporting other organizations, the more you will grow your reputation as a lawyer and a business.

Depending on the nature of the event, you can personally participate, or you can ask employees or proxies to participate. If it is an event likely to draw potential clients, offer a free intake (I say intake rather than consultation because we are talking about a brief screen, not a deeply individualized assessment). Participants can fill out an interest form with their contact information and some basic information about their case, and you can review them later to follow up with any potential clients. You can be present to meet people and offer to follow up with those who express an interest. You can have a raffle, where people fill out their contact info to win a prize. All of the email addresses collected can go on your newsletter list. This is a way to quickly build up an email list and following.

Look for organizations that align with your values and work. My firm partners with an organization in Richmond called the Blue Sky Fund, which provides transformational programming for young people through outdoor adventure programs and field trips for students in our city's public schools. I chose the organization because it aligns with my personal values, because I think nature-based learning and outdoor play and adventure is critical for children. It also aligns with our work and firm values because it promotes equal access to programs for public school students, including those in economically disadvantaged neighborhoods. The organization's work isn't controversial and doesn't implicate political or religious views, so our firm's support does not conflict with any employees' individual values or alienate clients. When a business supports an organization, there are opportunities to cross-promote, bringing attention to the organization as well as to your firm. It lets people know more about your business's values—and shows that you walk the walk on those values.

NEWSLETTER

A firm newsletter is a great way to share information and stay on people's radar. Do newsletters annoy some people? Maybe, but they can unsubscribe if they want. There are various platforms you can use to create newsletters. We use MailChimp and find it cost-effective. Start off by uploading all of your email contacts to the newsletter list. Don't overthink it. If it goes to someone off-target, they can unsubscribe. I find many people are actually genuinely interested and, if given the option, do want to receive a newsletter. The newsletter can be brief, but it should be regular. I recommend monthly, which is frequent enough and regular, but not overkill. Make sure you are including valuable content alongside self-promotion. Some people advocate for a ninety-ten ratio—90 percent true value, 10 percent sales/ask. For a law firm newsletter, it's enough to highlight the types of cases you handle.

The tone of the newsletter should be engaging. We use our newsletter to share changes in the law that may impact our clients or readers in general. We also use it to introduce new team members, share client testimonials and success stories, and highlight our practice areas,—particularly when we add a new case type to our practice. If you are starting out solo, I suggest you set aside two or three hours toward the end of the month to write your newsletter, and then send it out on the first of the next month. As you scale, this is a perfect task to delegate to a virtual assistant.

Marketing is one of the topics that most intimidates new business owners. The important takeaways are: 1) marketing is necessary; 2) marketing can and should evolve; and 3) a multi-prong approach is most effective. A strong digital presence, engaging video content, active social media, personal networking, and community engagement will transform you from a lawyer into a profitable business. The more people who know about you, the more clients you can serve. Now that you have the framework in place to attract a steady stream of clients to your firm, you need to ensure that you are setting fees properly to maximize your firm's profit.

CHAPTER 7

SETTING YOUR FEES

Public perception may be that lawyers are wealthy, but I have seen many lawyers significantly under-earning, especially when you consider the level of responsibility and professional duty we take on for clients. Based on my experience, there is a real risk among women attorneys to undercharge for a number of reasons. Traditionally, women have not been expected to earn well, and we have not been celebrated for being high earners and building wealth the same way as men. Even today, I have known professional women with successful husbands to say things like, "We don't really need my income" or "I don't really need to make that much money." Huh? Who doesn't like making money? Isn't two million better than one million? This isn't a hobby; you are running a business.

You know what you can do with a lot of money? You can give your kids the life you want for them—schools, camps, travel, ballet lessons, a house with a beautiful yard. You can contribute to your family's security by paying off your home, or saving for college, or building a comfortable retirement for you and your spouse. You can expand your business, create new jobs, and be a generous leader. You can donate money to amazing charities, or sponsor scholarships, or invest in other women entrepreneurs. You can also book yourself spa treatments, buy nice clothes, upgrade your champagne tastes, fly first class... It doesn't matter if you're a single mom and it's all on you, or if you're married to a successful partner who also earns a great living. Your income-earning ability is not contingent on someone else. You can excel in your own right, and together with your team and your family, you can enjoy the fruits of your labor. I had a law school professor who said, "You can do well and do good at the same time." Stop selling yourself short. Stop saying things like "we don't really need my income." The world needs your talent, and more money will make everything you want to do in life that much easier.

Women are often viewed in nurturing/caregiving roles. Our job is to take care of people, not to support them or ourselves. Women—even highly educated ones with great earning potential—are socialized (brainwashed?) into feeling guilty for focusing on money. Wanting to make a lot of money (if you're a woman, at least) means you're greedy. If we really care about other people, we will want to help them out of the kindness of our hearts, not because we want to make money. Even within the legal profession, women charge less or even work for free because they "feel bad" or "just want to help." Clients may bring these preconceived ideas with them, as well. Once, an older client actually asked me why I needed to charge "so much" if I was married. Though these attitudes do exist externally, I sometimes think we are our own worst enemies when it comes to demanding our own value.

Reject the myth that wanting to make a lot of money is greedy.

Reject the caregiver myth that women should always put others' needs above our own. Get over all of that right now. Stop perpetuating the tropes that we are supposed to do our work out of the goodness of our hearts, while men get to make money from it. I *love* being a lawyer, and I assume you do, too. I remember watching courtroom dramas at my grandparents' house as a young child (*Matlock*, anyone?) and thinking, wow, I want to do that. I read *To Kill a Mockingbird* and knew that someday I wanted to stand up in a courtroom and speak up for another person facing injustice. In my years of practice, I have had the honor of representing clients in incredible cases; and I know you have, too. We didn't enter the legal profession as a get-rich-quick scheme. On challenging days, I can think of much easier ways to earn a good living. Law is a noble profession that requires us to shoulder incredible levels of responsibility and stress for other human beings. We *are* caregivers and we *do* have big hearts, and that is part of what makes us amazing attorneys. We deserve to charge for the incredible services we provide and to be compensated for the important work we do.

DITCH HOURLY FEES

Fees should either be flat fee or contingency fee, depending on the case type. The hourly billing practice is incredibly dumb, and everyone should stop doing it immediately. Keeping time in six-minute increments is ridiculous. That's just no way to live. It is also stressful to clients to not know how much they are incurring in fees until the end of the month. Put yourself in the consumer's position—would you rather someone say "this service costs $5,000" or "I don't know how much this service will cost. I'll let you know at the end of each month how much you owe me, and we'll see how it goes." Hourly fees do not promote efficiency, expertise, or expediency. The practice actually punishes lawyers who draw on their knowledge, experience, and professional reputation to promptly and painlessly resolve legal matters for their clients. The hourly billing hurts both lawyers and clients because it rewards inefficiency. This makes no sense, and it's not fair to anyone.

The value to a client comes in the quality of the service you provide to the client, in your experience and expertise, and in the outcome—not in the number of hours you spend on it. Do you think your client cares if you spent one hour or fifty hours on a case, if you provided excellent representation and achieved a favorable outcome? As you advance in your career—or you may already be there—your knowledge and experience will enable you to spend less time on a matter. As you grow your team, you will be able to leverage other roles in your firm and delegate work to increase efficiency.

I advocate for flat fees based largely on value to the client. Legal ethics require that fees be reasonable and take into account certain factors, like the difficulty or novelty of a legal issue. However, there is a really broad range of fees that could be considered acceptable. Think about the value that you are giving a client. Yes, it is relevant to consider the time and office resources a matter will require. You are going to charge more for a felony case that could go to a jury trial than you would for a traffic ticket. But *what* we offer to clients is exceptionally important, not just the number of hours worked. Your flat fee can take into account, among other things, your experience and expertise.

As a starting point, your fee should reflect the gravity of the situation you are handling for the client. If you have a lot of experience in a particular case type and a history of success, that increases the value of your service. If your office has stream-lined processes and excellent customer service, that increases the value to the client, too, because they are getting faster results and better client care. My office has very experienced support staff and efficient workflows, which allow us to file cases quickly. One case type we handle has a strict filing deadline and tends to require emergency hearings, so we have developed systems in place where we can commit to filing that particular case type within the same *week* a client hires us. That factor alone adds significantly to the value we offer.

If you have some semi-predictable costs associated with certain case types, I strongly recommend you roll them into your fee. Everyone prefers having a single fee to pay rather than multiple invoices or unpredictable costs. Don't overthink it—you do not need to bill a client for every penny. If you have fairly predict-able costs to a case, take them into consideration when you set your fee. For example, if you know that a certain case type will require you to request medical records, factor that into your fee. In your representation agreement, state that "fees include obtaining necessary medical records." If you know a case will require a $100 filing fee, factor that into your fee. In your repre-sentation agreement, say "filing fees included." It does not need to be an exact science. It doesn't matter if the records cost $275 in one case and $310 in another case, because they are business expenses to you, and you are building them into your fee *generally*. You are factoring in costs to ensure that your fees are profitable, and you are giving your clients the benefit of paying a single, fixed bill so they don't need to worry about unexpected invoices. You are saving yourself administrative time and effort by avoid-ing generating multiple invoices and collecting payments, and you are reducing stress in the attorney-client relationship. No one likes getting a bill from a lawyer, so make it one and done.

KNOW YOUR VALUE

I strongly recommend taking time to work on your mindset and attitudes toward money. Here is a personal anecdote. For several years, I was charging $5,000 for a particular case type I handle. It is a very time-intensive case type, one that requires individualized research and writing for each case. Over time, I gradually raised my fee to $7,500, then eventually to $10,000. Each time I raised the fee, I convinced myself no one would hire me at that rate. I would feel nervous each time I quoted a consultation, and slightly amazed each time someone went for it.

To be clear, these fees were, if anything, unreasonably *low*. But it took me several years to work up the nerve to raise my fees. Two years ago, as part of a consulting exercise, I reviewed all of my fees to see if they were appropriate. I knew that $10,000 was not nearly enough for the amount of time and effort that went into that case type, but again, I was nervous to raise the fee. I finally bit the bullet and raised the fee to $25,000.

Soon after, the day came for my first consultation where I would be quoting that fee to someone. As soon as I said the fee, I immediately convinced myself there was no way they would go for it. The client picked up her purse and I knew she was about to walk out. Except...she didn't walk out. She opened up her purse and took out her checkbook and wrote a check for the full fee right then and there! I was in shock. She looked...relieved, happy even. Who would be happy about writing a $25,000 check to a lawyer?

Well, it turned out that she had previously hired a different lawyer for the case (one who did not specialize in the case type, and who I knew had less experience than me). His fee? It was $50,000! But he had messed up and not filed on time, so he returned her money, and she hired me. She had paid $50,000 for the same case type, and I—the lawyer with a successful track record—charged *half* of that. *Half* the fee of a man who actually almost screwed up the case.

Sit down and make a list of the types of cases you handle. If you handle multiple practice areas or case types, try to group relevant ones together. Be honest with yourself about what they are worth. Look at the value you are giving to a client in that case—not just the outcome, which we typically can't guarantee, but the overall value. Set a flat fee that reflects the gravity and value of your work. You explain complicated concepts. You draw on your experience and advise on the best course of action in a confusing situation. You think creatively to solve a stressful problem. You fight for your client, so that even if the outcome is less than favorable, that client knows you did everything possible for them. Only generally consider the time you spend; don't trade dollars for hours. Think about all of the energy that goes into a case—it's not just the court appearances or the legal writing. Client calls, emails, questions, handholding, and minor hiccups all add time and energy to a case.

You can take into consideration "market rate" fees if you want, but don't limit yourself to what other people charge. They may not give the same value as you, or they may be wildly off-base in their fees. I have seen lawyers charge $2,500 to $50,000 for the same type of case. I have had clients leave another law firm charging a third of what we charge and hire us because they believe it is a better service.

The number you come up with should be a significant reflection of the value you give to a client. It's okay if it sounds expensive. You're a top-notch attorney, not the dollar store.

As you set your fees, keep the following considerations in mind.

DO NOT DECIDE FOR YOUR PROSPECTIVE CLIENTS WHAT THEY CAN AFFORD.

Resist this trap. You have no idea what your prospective clients can afford. It's none of your business. Even if you have their bank statement sitting in front of you, you still don't know where your fee might come from. You are setting appropriate fees for excellent legal service. Your first job is to explain the value to prospective clients so that they *want* to hire you (more on this shortly). It's their decision whether they can afford it and how.

I was once working with a client on his wife's immigration case. At the time, my fee for that case type was $3,500. I was worried about the client's ability to pay. Not only did he hire, but he casually mentioned that he had just spent $3,000 on a *fortune teller* to have her predict the outcome of the wife's case. True story.

It was not my job to decide whether that man had $3,500 or whether he wanted to spend it on his wife's legal case. It was my job to set the fee and provide a valuable service. Fortunately, he was agreeable to that fee. He also spent almost the same amount of money to have his palm read by a fortune teller. As the saying goes, don't count other people's money.

DO NOT SET YOUR FEES BASED ON YOUR COLLEAGUES' FEES FOR FEAR OF COMPETITION.

Worry about your own fees and the service you provide. Remember the guy who charged $50,000? Was he worried about losing business to me because I charged $25,000? No, he wasn't, and the client actually hired him first. I know lawyers who charge *one-tenth* of what my firm charges for particular case types. Are we losing business? No. We've grown in size and revenue each and every year since I first opened a law firm.

Do not engage in a race to the bottom. Charging appropriately enables us to do better work. It allows us to hire more support staff, which enables us to be more responsive, spend more time preparing a case, file things more quickly, and invest in newer technology for client convenience. Maybe the guy next door charges half of what you charge. If you are providing a valuable service and communicate that to prospective clients, people will hire you.

DO NOT UNDERVALUE OR DISCOUNT YOURSELF.

Something that I have noticed both as a lawyer and as a consumer is that women tend to discount themselves—even when no one asks. You're sitting in a consultation, and you're about to quote the fee. You really want to ask for $10,000 because you know this is an important case and will take a lot of work. You open your mouth, and $7,500 pops out. Why? You doubted yourself. You convinced yourself the client couldn't afford $10,000. You were afraid she would leave and hire someone else who charges less.

Or maybe, you stuck to your guns and quoted the appropriate fee, and the client said, "Wow, that's a lot of money. Is there any way you can do it for less?" And you said, "Well, I can discount it to $7,500..."

I encourage you to set and stick to a fee—do not undervalue yourself, and do not reduce your value for clients. Many lawyers, particularly in small firms, take what I believe is a very unprofessional approach to fees. They barter or negotiate, or change their fees depending on the client or the day of the week. Your fees are your fees. You don't go into a store and negotiate prices. When your CPA sends you the bill for your tax preparation, you don't reply and say, "Hey, this is a lot, and I've had a rough month. Can you take off a few hundred dollars?" When you get your mortgage statement, you don't say, "You know, this month I think I'll just pay $1,000, because I'm under a lot of stress." When you go to the hair salon, their prices are fixed. The stylist doesn't look at you and think, what a nice lady, I'm going to help her out and reduce the rate for a haircut.

You have fixed bills to pay, and so should your clients. Take out the negotiation, guesswork, and unpredictability. Set your fees and do not discount them.

SET YOUR LIST, SAVE IT, AND STICK TO IT.

If you have another team member(s) handling intake or payments, make sure they have your list of fees. Do not make exceptions. No exception for the really nice man who mentions four times in the consultation that he's short on money. No exception for the friend of a friend of a friend of someone you represented eight years ago who really wants to hire you but is out of work. *It's okay if someone can't afford to hire you.* It's okay if a product or service is out of someone's price range.

I have found that the more value you provide in your services, and the better you get at communicating that value (see Chapter 8 on consultations and sales), the more people will surprise you and hire you. But not everyone will. Sometimes people call my office for a free consultation. I don't do free consultations for most case types. Occasionally, someone will want to hire but they say they can only pay X amount per month, less than one of our offered payment plans. If that is truly the case, then we are not a good fit for each other.

When you discount your fees for one client, you are undervaluing yourself in a few ways. One, you are telling that client that your fees and boundaries are negotiable, and that *they* get to determine your value. Two, you are robbing your own business of revenue, which impacts you as well as anyone who works for you. Three, you are compromising firm resources away from your other paying clients. Finally, I have found through experience that clients who haggle over fees are going to be difficult clients in other ways. These clients tend not to respect your professional boundaries or value your time and work. Your law office is not a yard sale where someone walks in and says "I'll give you $5 for this." You cannot run a successful and profitable business by having clients pay what they want, which is essentially what you are doing when you negotiate and discount fees.

BE PREPARED WHEN YOU MEET WITH POTENTIAL CLIENTS.

Go into a consultation with a prepared representation agreement and your fee list at your fingertips. If you offer a single case type, that should be easy. I have multiple practice areas and case types, so we keep an electronic folder in our system with various engagement letters and our fee list handy. If a client is ready to hire on the spot, the attorney can send it to the printer and a staff member brings it into the conference room. If it's a virtual consultation, it can be sent electronically during or immediately after the consultation. Having it prepared in writing makes it less tempting to negotiate, and it signals to the potential client that it is a set policy.

> For sample scripts on explaining fees in a clear and client-forward way and for handling common objections to fees, go to www.momsalawyer.com.

ACCEPTING PAYMENTS

My rule of thumb is this: make it as easy as possible for people to pay you. You've set your fee, you've engaged the client, and it's time for them to pay. Give them multiple ways to do so easily.

In today's market, you need to take credit cards. A 2020 study by the US Federal Reserve concluded that 86 percent of Americans have at least one credit card.[23] For purposes of this conversation, I put credit and debit cards together; from a payment-processing perspective, it makes no difference. It is very easy to take credit card payments, and you absolutely must be set up to do so from Day One. My firm uses LawPay for several reasons. One, it syncs with Clio, a client management software we use to track client accounts. Two, because it is set up for both operating and escrow deposits—which is very important for lawyers, because certain funds need to be deposited into escrow in order to comply with state bar requirements. Three, it is competitive in terms of processing fees. You can send clients payment links, set up automatic payment plans, and embed payment links on your website.

Credit card processing fees can be a touchy subject in law firm management. Credit card processing companies charge fees for credit card payments. The fee is usually 1–4 percent of the cost. Some companies, including law firms, charge the client a processing fee. If you are going to do this, check your state bar rules for compliance. In my state, you can do it as long as it is explained to the client that there is an additional charge.

I have taken various approaches to this over the years but reached the conclusion that it's just a business cost. Do not charge clients an extra 2 percent to use their credit card. As a consumer, I don't like feeling nickeled and dimed. It annoyed me when airlines started charging us separately for checking bags. I prefer to have a single fee to pay, which encompasses the business costs. In other words, consider that credit card processing fees are a cost of doing business in the same way that buying printer paper or having the Internet is. If you were thinking of charging $2,500 for a case type, consider making that $2,750, and it will more than cover your costs. From a client service standpoint, that is a smoother approach than saying your fee is $2,500, but if you're paid with a credit card you need to charge $72 more. It also removes the bookkeeping issue of charging a card and making sure the legal fee goes into escrow and the processing fee goes into operating—which is, frankly, annoying and not worth it.

To reduce costs (to you and the client) encourage clients to pay via a direct transfer from their checking account, or ACH (automated clearinghouse). This is a direct payment from the client's bank account to yours without the credit card company as a middle man. Many vendors I use in my business require I pay them through ACH, and it's very simple. The client provides their banking information and authorization to charge, just as they would fill out their credit card information for a payment. It removes the extra fees, saving you that cost. As your revenue grows, you will be saving yourself thousands of dollars in operating costs by processing payments through ACH versus credit card. LawPay is set up to handle ACH payments without the additional fees associated with credit or debit cards.

We present clients with payment information via ACH, and many pay that way without question. If a client specifically requests to pay via card, we accept that, too. You want to balance saving costs where you can, while also always making it easy for people to hire and pay you. Depending on the demographics of your clientele, some clients may want to send in checks or even come in person to pay. In sum, set your fees to account for various business costs, and use the most cost-effective methods when available. But make it easy for clients to pay you.

PAYMENT PLANS

If you follow my advice and charge flat fees for any non-contingency work, people are going to ask if you offer payment plans. My advice is simple: for fees over a certain amount, offer specific payment plans without exception.[24] I have experimented with different approaches over the years and landed on what has been a very successful payment plan system that is mutually beneficial to the firm and to clients. Currently, we offer three options on fees above a certain amount: Plan A) pay in full; Plan B) 30 percent down payment (+$500) and three monthly payments; Plan C) 30 percent down payment (+$1,000) and six monthly payments. The payment plans cost more, because we are not receiving payment in full and bear the administrative costs of monitoring the payment plans.

Here is an example for a flat fee case type of $10,000:

Plan A: $10,000 paid in full

Plan B: $10,500—$3,800 down and 3 monthly payments of $2,223.33

Plan C: $11,000—$4,300 down and 6 monthly payments of $1,116.66

At the consultation, we provide the potential client with a representation agreement and a clear explanation of the three different payment plan options. *Payment plans must be on automatic payments—no exceptions.* If a client elects Plan B or Plan C, they can make the down payment in any form they wish, but all subsequent payments must be on ACH or credit/debit card with a signed authorization to auto-debit or auto-charge each month until paid in full.

Present the payment plans in a professional way with no room for negotiation or exceptions. You are responsible for generating consistent revenue in your business. You are responsible for setting and demanding your own value. If someone needs and wants your services, it is their responsibility to manage their finances so as to be able to hire you. Allowing money-related negotiation into your attorney-client relationship can sour the entire dynamic. Do you want to spend time hounding clients to make payments? No. Set your fees, offer a reasonable payment plan, and leave it at that.

Many small firm lawyers convince themselves that *their* clients would never be able to afford higher fees, or would never opt for payment plans with automatic payments. I can tell you that's not true. Most of our firm's clients are not wealthy people. We represent people from across different backgrounds and income levels. Clients not only accept, but *appreciate,* when a law firm is professional and transparent in its fees. Do you know any other professional businesses that barter, or accept "pay what you can," or take monthly payments whenever it's convenient to the customer? Don't make assumptions and underestimate your clients. Be a professional in your offerings and your requirements. If you're offering payment plans and multiple methods of payment, someone who wants and needs to hire you will hire you. Don't reduce your value and participate in a race to the bottom. If another firm wants to take $100 a month for four years, or chase down clients to get payments, let them. You'll be busy working on new business while enjoying paid-in-full accounts and consistent monthly cash flow.

Once you have established your fee list, payment plans, and invoicing procedures, you are ready to intake new clients.

CHAPTER 8

INTAKING CLIENTS

In *Career and Family: Women's Century-Long Journey toward Equity*, Harvard economist Claudia Goldin traces the history of women specifically in professional fields and explains why equality remains elusive. I highly recommend this book for a deep dive into the historical view of how professional women have struggled to combine work and family over the past century. The research is validating—the deck is still stacked against us, but not for the reasons some may think.

Today, we have anti-discrimination laws; women are attaining the same educational levels in the same or higher numbers, and social attitudes have widely evolved. Yet, women attorneys still report significantly higher levels of stress and dissatisfaction. Why? Because the entire system of work, particularly professional work, is entirely incompatible with having a family. Goldin points to law as a particular example of what she calls "greedy" work: professions that demand time and attention to the exclusion of personal or family life. Traditional law fits squarely into the category, with its toxic culture of long hours, need for perpetual email access, and competition, all in a field that is already inherently stressful because of the responsibilities owed to clients. Our work culture has evolved into something so demanding that it is virtually *impossible* for two parents to work and raise kids. As a result, women either have to step down in their careers, as Goldin writes, or they burn out and develop a drinking problem, as the ABA reports.

The good news? We're changing that. Maybe you were in that world, and you left. Maybe you took a peek at that world, and said no, thank you. Maybe you're still in law school and you already know that's not for you. Maybe the pandemic is what made you see the light—that craziness wasn't working out. But that's in the past, because together we are opening and running law firms that will change things from the inside.

We've already talked about setting boundaries around your schedule and your fees, but it's equally important to set up systems for dealing with clients so that you can work efficiently and effectively—and maintain your boundaries in the process. We also want our firms to be profitable, by maintaining consistently growing revenue.

INTAKE

It is absolutely imperative that you have a streamlined and accessible intake process. You need to make it as easy as possible for a potential client to find you and communicate their needs to your firm. The first interaction between your firm and a potential caller should inspire confidence and reassurance, and begin to build trust.

So what does intake mean, exactly? I define intake as an initial screening of a potential client that does not involve legal advice. During intake, the intake professional is getting enough information for the firm to assess whether the caller is actually a potential client. This saves time and money. The intake professional will get basic contact information and a brief description of the case according to a script and guidelines you prepare. With proper training, an intake professional can determine whether it is an appropriate case for the firm. For example, if someone calls my office to find out if I prepare wills, my intake department can quickly determine that the caller is not a potential client for us and refer them to a trusted colleague. This saves our time, as well as the caller's time and money, because they are not coming in for a paid consultation. On the other hand, if someone calls in and reports that they were charged with a crime in our city, our intake department quickly identifies this person as a potential client, confirms to the caller that we do handle their case type, and schedules the next available consultation with an attorney. Intake should be tailored not just by practice area, but also case type. Our firm handles some types immigration cases, but not others. If someone calls in looking for an immigration lawyer, our intake department is trained to ask questions to identify if the caller has a case type we handle, or if we need to refer to a colleague with that specialization.

I suggest having multiple methods for potential clients to contact you. A contact/intake form on your website is a no-brainer. Make sure the intake forms are going to a central email address that is checked regularly.

If you have a true solo practice with no other employees, consider how to ensure that phone inquiries are handled promptly. If you are not ready for a full-time employee to answer calls, look at virtual employees. I have used virtual contractors at various points in my business growth. For example, Get Staffed Up is a legal staffing company based in Florida. The company is run by lawyers, so they are versed in law firm needs. Thanks to exchange rates, a virtual assistant overseas is much more cost-effective than an in-office employee, and the staffing company will handle the taxes and ensure compliance. As I began to hire staff in my office, I also utilized virtual staffers as receptionists. If that expense doesn't make sense for you immediately, another even more affordable option is a reception service. I will caution you that this is not a perfect solution. A virtual receptionist through a service is not an employee, so they are not going to be deeply familiar with your business. They will essentially follow a script and take down messages for you. This is not an ideal long-term solution, because you want the person answering calls to be a salesperson for your firm. In the beginning, however, the first step is to make sure your phones are being answered. Having a real person answer your phone, make a good first impression, and take down intake information, is preferable to voicemail.

When a caller is identified as a potential client, the role of the intake professional is to begin to cultivate a relationship between the potential client and the firm by letting the caller know we are interested in their case and scheduling a consultation promptly so we can learn more about the case and how we can help. Intake is standard procedure in some practice areas, and less common in others. Don't overthink this. Whoever is doing your intake should be familiar with your firm practice areas, values, and ideal clients. Train them sufficiently so they can inspire confidence in potential clients before they even come in for a consultation. You can have a catch-all provision to offer a consultation if the intake professional is unsure about whether a caller is a potential client.

CONSULTATIONS

If you are coming from a direct representation position, you may have experience with consultations. If so, forget what you know about lawyer consultations. If you are coming from a role where you did not handle consultations, forget whatever ideas you have about them. A consultation is *not*:

1. a three-hour meeting to discuss the potential client's entire life history.
2. a lengthy strategy session to discuss how you will handle every aspect of the case.
3. an opportunity for you and the potential client to get to know each other and form a deep bond.
4. a time for you to tell war stories.
5. a mini law school lesson where you identify all legal issues in the case and show off your knowledge and prowess.

A consultation should be a relatively short meeting where the potential client shares enough information confidentially for you to determine and communicate the answers to the following three questions to the potential client:

1. Can you help them?
2. How much will it cost them?
3. What is the next step?

I owe this philosophy of consultations to a colleague, Alexandra Lozano. For years, I was doing consultations by checking off every single item on the "what not to do" list until she showed me how to do it. Let me explain clearly why each of those items belongs on the don't-do-this list.

1. A three-hour meeting to discuss the potential client's entire life history. This is not necessary. It is very unlikely that your client's entire life history is relevant to the case. In limited circumstances, it may become relevant later. If so, you will have an opportunity *after they have hired you* to do a deep dive into their childhood or their first marriage or how they were treated three jobs ago.

2. A lengthy strategy session to discuss how you will handle every aspect of the case. It is not possible to do this in a helpful way at this early stage. You are only hearing your potential client's perspective of the case. If you've been a lawyer for more than two days, you will know that a client's perception of the case is only part of what you will ultimately need to know. It's a waste of time to fully flesh out a mistaken identity and alibi defense if in two weeks you're going to receive in discovery close-up surveillance footage of your client robbing the convenience store wearing a uniquely distinctive hat later found in their car (*cough cough* just an example; this has *definitely* never happened to me). Get an overview of the facts as a starting point, but save the case strategy for when you are hired and have access to more information. Building it now is a waste of time, as I've said, and the client will not let you forget what you "promised" in your initial assessment.

3. An opportunity for you and the potential client to get to know each other and form a deep bond. It sounds nice, but it's not necessary, and it's premature at the consultation. You want to inspire confidence by being professional, respectful, and reassuring. If this person hires you, you and your team will get to know them. This isn't a date, and you don't know for sure you will ever see them again.

4. A time for you to tell war stories. We all have them, and we all love sharing them. For the most part, the only people

who may enjoy lawyer war stories are other lawyers, so save it for the bar association cocktail party. Simply reassuring the potential client that you have handled many similar cases is enough to let them know you have experience. If you have impressive case results, put them up on your website or social media, and potential clients will read about them there.

5. A mini law school lesson where you identify all legal issues in the case, explain to the potential client, and show off your knowledge and prowess. Again, no one cares. People are coming to you with a problem that needs a solution. You can't identify all legal issues at the consultation, anyway (see item #2). You can inspire confidence without boring the person to death with case citations. If someone is actually interested, or innocent enough to ask a lawyer to pontificate on a legal theory, they will ask and *then* you can explain.

I believe in consultation fees. We charge consultation fees for most case types. The only exception is if the case type is one which will be a contingency fee. If a case is going to be a flat fee (because we're only doing flat fees, not hourly—remember?), we charge a consultation fee that must be paid to confirm the appointment and go on the calendar. There are a few reasons to do this. One, you are spending time in the consultation. Two, you are providing value whether they hire you or not. Three, you are signaling to the potential client that your time and work has value. Again and again over the years, I have found that when consultations are free, potential clients treat them less seriously. You will get no-shows, or people shopping around who are not serious about retaining. Your calendar will fill up with consultations with people looking for free advice who have no real intention or means to hire you. How many times have you signed up for a free webinar and blown it off? Have you ever done that with a webinar that cost $250? Some lawyers do free consultations. Since we are not concerning ourselves with what other lawyers do, but what is best for our business, charge a consultation fee.

Consultations should be streamlined. If you are following an intake procedure, most consultations should be viable leads. If you have vetted the basic compatibility of the potential client, screened and referred out cases outside of your practice area, and charged an appropriate consultation fee, almost everyone coming in for a consultation should be a viable client. You are not beginning to work on the case at a consultation, because the client has not hired you yet. The consultation is a time to identify whether you can help this client, and then to convey to them your terms so they can decide if they want to hire you. You need a brief description of the matter, and then you identify the central issue and whether it is an issue you can assist with. You then explain the basic trajectory of the case, the fees, and the next steps.

Here are a few examples of what the conversation might look like.

Example 1: The potential client shares that she wants to separate from her husband. They own a house, two vehicles, and retirement accounts. They both work and have two minor children.

After she has given you this information, you are in a position to explain the following: "I can help you navigate your separation and divorce. A divorce can be resolved through settlement or through court. We will look at all of your assets and debts, and determine a fair way to divide them. We will discuss what type of custody arrangement would be in the best interests of the children, based on several factors that the law requires us to consider. There are laws in place to protect both parties in a divorce. We can then propose a settlement to your husband's attorney. We may negotiate back and forth to reach something you both agree on. If we reach an agreement, we file the paperwork in court and typically after about six months, you will be divorced. If you absolutely cannot agree, then we have the option of filing a divorce complaint in court and scheduling a hearing for the judge to hear both sides and make a decision on how your property will be distributed and custody arranged. That process usually takes closer to a year, because we need to get on the court's schedule. My fee for a divorce is $X. When you are ready to retain us, the first step will be to sign the representation agreement and arrange the payment. Then we will sit down and review all of the financial information and discuss different options for child custody. We will help you navigate this entire process as smoothly and painlessly as possible."

What You Did → You reassured the potential client that you can help her navigate this stressful situation, and you conveyed knowledge of her issue. You controlled the conversation and limited it to what information is necessary at this stage in the representation. You described the basic process so she knows what to expect. You explained your fees and the next step.

What You Didn't Do → You did not sit and listen to all of her grievances about her husband. You did not speculate about how a court would award custody after hearing only one side of the story. You did not sit and calculate child support and her likely financial settlement based on incomplete information. You did not make any promises or scare her off with tough love. You explained the legal process, but you did not begin working on the case prior to being retained.

In other words, you answered these questions:

Can you help? Yes.

How much will it cost? $X fee.

What is the next step? Hiring you, providing financial information, and drafting a settlement proposal for the other party.

You may be thinking, this lady has no clue what it's like to do a divorce consultation. There's going to be crying and noseblowing, and I need a minimum of two hours to get through all of the information. But stay with me. Everything I'm advising you to do, I do myself and have learned through practice. I promise it's possible. You need to train yourself to stay on script and control the consultation.

Example 2: The potential client is starting a new business and wants to trademark her company name and slogan. She explains that she's launching a lifestyle brand and plans to use the company name in several different ways.

"Your new brand sounds amazing! I can definitely assist you in applying for a trademark. We will file the trademark application, which will then be reviewed by the US Patent & Trademark Office. They can approve it, or they may request additional information from us before making a decision. The entire process usually takes between twelve and eighteen months. I offer a flat fee package for $X that covers a clearance search, trademark application, and certificate delivery. Once we onboard you as a client, we will immediately begin with the clearance search to make sure the trademark is available, and our goal is to file the application within three weeks."

What You Did → You reassured the potential client that you can help her apply for a trademark, and you conveyed knowledge of the process. You controlled the conversation and limited it to what information is necessary at this stage in the representation. You described the basic process so she knows what to expect. You explained your fees and the next step.

What You Didn't Do → You did not discuss the details of her business or her future plans for the trademark, or advise her on how she could change her name to improve her chances of approval. You did not describe in depth every possible challenge you may receive to the trademark and how you would handle each hypothetical challenge. You did not offer to do a clearance search before hiring. You explained the legal process, but you did not begin working on the case prior to being retained.

Can you help? Yes.

How much will it cost? $X fee.

What is the next step? Hiring you, so you can begin with a clearance search to make sure the trademark is available before preparing an application.

In both of these scenarios, you are giving value to the client by reassuring them that you can help, and explaining the basic legal process. Most clients are not experienced in legal matters, and the unknown adds to stress. They may have heard incorrect information or read a crazy article on the internet.

The first step is reassurance. Yes, you can help them with this issue. You're not *guaranteeing* an *outcome*, but you are *assuring* them that you can help guide them through their legal issue.

The second step is basic information. Do not underestimate the value of this. A client going through a divorce may have absolutely no idea what to expect. Who decides child custody? Who gets the house? By explaining that you can work toward a mutually agreeable settlement, you are letting her know that she is going to have some control in the situation. By explaining that if settlement fails, she can go to court, you are letting her know that there are safeguards in place if the other party is unreasonable. By estimating the time frame and explaining your fees, you are taking some of the mystery out of things. This is exactly the value that is appropriate before you are retained.

After you are retained, it is then appropriate to gather information and give specific advice on strategy and likely outcomes. You can't do this in the initial consultation because you don't have enough information (even if you let the client talk for three hours, you won't have enough information). You shouldn't do this in the initial consultation because you have not been hired yet.

REPRESENTATION AGREEMENTS

Execute written engagement agreements with clients in every case. Not all states require written representation agreements, but there is no reason not to have one. It is best practice, makes sure everyone is on the same page, and avoids conflicts. In a worst-case scenario, it can protect you in case of a dispute (but I can't think of a single time in my experience it has ever even come to that). Review your representation agreements at least once a year to see if revisions are needed. As you hire intake and onboarding staff, confer with them to see if there are any commonly asked questions that could be succinctly addressed in the agreement.

However, don't over-lawyer it. There is no need for a ten-page document outlining every possible scenario that could conceivably arise in the course of your representation. Resist the lawyerly urge to dream up every possible issue that could plausibly occur. In nearly fifteen years of practice, I have had very few questions, let alone conflicts, in my representation agreements.

You should review your state professional rules of conduct for compliance, but there are a couple of things I recommend including no matter what. The highlights are this: short description of the matter ("representation on a charge of assault and battery in Richmond General District Court" or "representation on citizenship application"), the fees ("$5,000 fee"), and a brief statement on how the fees are earned ("fees are earned for work provided, and the fee will be earned in full upon filing of the application").

Try to keep your representation agreement to one page. The purpose is to clearly and succinctly inform clients of the terms of your representation so that everyone understands the scope of work, the fees, and how the fees are earned. I firmly believe that representation agreements and the fees themselves should be as simple and as clear as possible. It's better for everyone if the terms are clearly understood in simple language.

For sample templates of representation agreements, go to www.momsalawyer.com.

Keep your representation agreements standardized. We are not reinventing the wheel for each case. Convert your representation agreement to be electronically signed. There are several companies that offer this service, the best known of which is probably Docusign. At my firm, I use a program called Eversign. It is easy to use and very inexpensive (plans range from free basic plans to professional plans for less than $100/month). When a client hires you, you can easily email a representation agreement and have a signed copy in moments. All parties get an emailed copy and signed confirmation.

AFTER THE CONSULTATION

At the consultation, you should be prepared for the potential client to hire on the spot. That means having a representation agreement on hand, and a way to process payments. If you are doing the consultation in person, you can bring a folder with a representation agreement and payment form. If you need to set the fee in the consultation, leave a blank line and write in the fee before handing it to the potential client at the end of the meeting. If you are doing a virtual consultation, have the representation agreement and payment link on hand to email to the client at the end of the consultation.

I strongly recommend having written materials explaining your fees. This looks professional and official. Verbal discussions on fees can seem less formal and are more likely to invite negotiation attempts (which you are not to entertain). It's also nice to have some very basic written materials or infographics outlining the process. When I consulted a trademark attorney, she sent me a simple flowchart of the different steps in the trademark process and approximate wait times. This helped me easily visualize the steps and timeframe. We do something similar in our office to help clients understand the steps in a case and the approximate timeframe. Handing a client some branded material at the end of a consultation is another opportunity to give the client some value and create a positive, professional, and knowledgeable impression.

Potential clients who do not immediately hire you should go into a follow-up funnel. There are several reasons why clients want to hire, but just not hire immediately. Some will want to discuss your fees with family, or wait until their next pay day, or just sleep on it. The follow-up process should be as systematic as possible. When you are first starting out and have a smaller number of consultations and clients, an easy way to ensure follow-up is to set calendar reminders after the consultation. Keep an email template with your representation agreement and payment link, and modify it as necessary. Follow-up should not be random. I suggest you begin follow-up within two days of the consultation if someone does not hire on the spot. If the case is urgent, include any terms you may have with respect to the hiring date. For example, if a potential client has a hearing date scheduled in two weeks, or a statute of limitations will expire in six months, what is the last date you need to be hired and paid in order to accept representation? For other matters, you should remain in contact with promising potential clients who do not hire right away. Invite them to follow your firm page on social media and add their email address to your newsletter list.

After the first two weeks following the consultation, add them to monthly follow-up/check-in emails. Potential clients can also be added to your email newsletter. Every consultation is a chance to make a positive impression and form a relationship. If they don't hire you now, they may hire down the road, or they might refer others to your firm.

The process of converting a potential client into an actual client has three steps: Intake, Consultation, and Follow-up/Sign-up. Every step in the process is an opportunity for you and your firm to inspire reassurance and give value to potential clients. It is important to remember that this process is a sales process, and a professional, streamlined approach is valuable to both you and your future clients.

At this point, your firm is operational, and you have systems in place to accept clients and generate revenue. This is an enormous accomplishment, and it is only the beginning.

CHAPTER 9

DEVELOPING PERSONALLY AND PROFESSIONALLY

If you haven't already, as soon as you finish this book, I want you to go read *We Should All be Millionaires* by Rachel Rodgers. This book is on my personal required reading list for women entrepreneurs. Rachel's passion is promoting success and financial wealth for women through entrepreneurship, and she challenges women to reject so many of the myths and traditional notions that have kept us from achieving significant wealth. One of the themes in Rachel's book that spoke most loudly to me was the idea that we do not need to operate in the old-school, male-centric workforce model to be successful.

And how do we build a new model? By not always putting ourselves last, and by taking time to develop both personally and professionally.

If professional development was important to you as a lawyer, consider it absolutely critical as a business owner. If you are like most practicing attorneys, you know next to nothing about running a profitable business. When I started my first law firm, I had none of the resources I needed to open and operate a business. So many lawyers ignore the business side of their firms. They think that opening a law firm is as simple as renting an office, throwing up a website, and waiting for the phone to start ringing. Then, if they do manage to attract any clients, they spend all of their time working on cases and going to court, and expect that their revenue will just steadily increase over time. I know that's exactly what I thought when I first "hung a shingle," as they say.

What helped me grow my law practice into a profitable business (meaning, a business that turns a profit after expenses) and evolve from a lawyer who happened to own a law practice into a business owner? Relentless professional development. There is more to professional development than signing up for a bunch of CLEs the month before the reporting deadline or attending the bar association holiday party. Professional development needs to be a daily commitment to learning everything about running a business so that you can respond to challenges and continuously grow and improve your business. Over time, our goal is to transform your role into an executive. In the beginning, you may be filling most or all of the roles in your firm. Professional development must be a priority from Day One.

NEVER STOP LEARNING

My suggestion is to begin by just consuming as much information as possible. There are a myriad of books, guides, podcasts, and webinars on every aspect of law firm and business management. Yes, there are a million things you have to learn about running a business. The good news is that there are a million resources out there. Start learning as much as you can, right now, about business structure, human resources, hiring, process creation, sales, customer service, finance and accounting... The list goes on.

At the end of this book is a list of some of my favorite books and podcasts that have helped me develop different aspects of my practice.

Take a few minutes to sit down with your phone and subscribe to at least five podcasts related to law firms, small business, and entrepreneurship. Your new hobby is listening to these whenever possible—in the car, while you travel, in your downtime. I play podcasts on my phone while I get ready in the morning, while I drive to work, and while I run.

Then, take a few more minutes to load up your e-reader (or your nightstand) with books. While I love buying physical books, for this purpose, I do prefer my e-reader because I can easily carry it with me all the time. Download several business books on your e-reader, slip it into your bag, and read instead of playing on your phone every chance you get—waiting in court, waiting for an oil change, or sitting in the school pick-up line.

While you are building up a knowledge base in these areas, you will come across various different communities. There are many Facebook groups, listservs, retreats, and trainings that are marketed to lawyers, law firm owners, and small business owners in general. Joining a group is a great way to learn from others, collaborate, and be held accountable as you are building your business. I recommend following a company or group for a while to see if it is the right fit for you. I have worked with several different coaching programs at various points in my journey. A typical trajectory goes something like this: hear about a book or author on a podcast ↬ read the book ↬ follow the person/company online ↬ see a webinar/training/event that speaks to an area I am looking to develop.

Here are a few concrete examples of how my constant information consumption helped me grow my firm.

In January 2020, I heard a guest named Brett Trembly on The Law Entrepreneur podcast talk about his new legal staffing company, Get Staffed Up. I was looking to hire an assistant but was nervous about adding another full-time position because I had hired three full-time employees in less than a year. I looked the company up and saw that they offered staffing for bilingual law firm administrative staff at very reasonable rates. I ended up working with the company to fill multiple positions in my firm, which allowed me to scale more quickly than I otherwise could have afforded. Beginning with virtual positions and scaling to in-office positions became an important strategy for my growth.

In 2018, I read a book called *The Game Changing Attorney* by Michael Mogill, the owner of Crisp, a law firm growth company specializing in video marketing. The book talks extensively about the importance of video and storytelling in marketing. I began following the company on social media. At the time, working with Crisp was out of my budget, but I continued to follow the company's offerings. In early 2020, Mogill launched a podcast under the same name, and I immediately subscribed. Later that same year, I signed on for a yearlong program with Crisp which helped me develop my current infrastructure. I also attend their yearly GameChangers conference for law firm owners focused on innovative law firm growth.

In a Facebook group for women lawyers, I saw members discussing hiring a CFO. At the time, I was responsible for handling most of the firm's finances—including paying bills, handling escrow transfers, and collecting client payments. It was a significant time commitment and increasingly stressful as the business grew. I had tried an online bookkeeping service, but it still required a lot of my time and did little to alleviate stress. I had a CPA who prepared our taxes each year, but he had nothing to do with the day-to-day bookkeeping. I had no idea that a small business could even have a CFO, but I was intrigued by the idea of having some expert assistance with firm finances.

I scheduled a consultation with Lydia Desnoyers at Premium Profit and was sold a few minutes into our conversation. Lydia is part CPA, part financial planner, part coach—she has helped me transform both the day-to-day finances and my long-term vision for the firm. Together, we have revamped our billing and invoicing systems, systemized our payment plans, improved efficiency and cost-saving, standardized employee compensation, and regulated revenue and projected cash flow. Lydia has advised me on several financial decisions for the firm and connected me with other vendors. All of this from a professional whose position I had never even heard of until I read a thread in a Facebook group several years into law firm ownership.

You do not need to spend thousands of dollars on professional development in the early days. Jump in on podcasts and books and learn as much as you can from multiple sources. Once you have a basic knowledge of your needs and the types of services out there, you can identify the right service to fit each need. For example, listen and read up on digital marketing to understand what other law firms are doing. Then, consult with a few different companies to understand average costs and offerings, and choose one that fits your needs and your budget. You can also start small and scale.

Take my marketing journey, for example. When I started my first firm, we had an extremely basic website and an even more basic Facebook page that I created myself. At that time, I knew absolutely nothing about law firm marketing. As I learned about video content, search engine optimization, and sales funnels, I upgraded my website and social media pages several times over the next few years. The first time I signed on with a marketing company, I was nervous to commit to the $750/month fee to maintain my website and social media (at the time, Facebook and Instagram pages). Eventually, I moved over to a more personalized service that included video production and content writing. Today, I have a full-time marketing and community engagement associate on my staff at the firm *and* a monthly contract with a digital marketing agency. We have a top-notch website, maintain professional social media accounts across all major platforms, produce a podcast, write a monthly newsletter, and participate in local community and virtual events. It was a gradual process to scale our marketing, but all along the way, I was learning everything I could about law firm marketing and technology.

It may take some time to find the right crew. There are many groups, courses, and masterminds that can give you a comprehensive introduction to different aspects of law firm management. Many of those are significant commitments that can cost thousands or tens of thousands of dollars, and I recommend exploring them so you can find the right fit, even if it feels aspirational at the moment. Remember that what we are doing takes a non-traditional approach in a very traditional field. While there is a lot of innovation in law firm management, this is still pretty cutting-edge. Law is light-years behind other fields in marketing and advertising. Many lawyers still associate marketing with "ambulance chasers," and many state bars have restrictive rules on marketing. Many small law "firms" are solo practitioners or loose partnerships of lawyers sharing an office. In other words, many people in your current professional circle may not understand, or may openly criticize, what you do. You need to be able to focus on your vision, tune out naysayers, and affiliate yourself as much as possible with people who are either doing what you want to do, or want to do the same things you want to do. For this reason, once you have developed a foundational comfort with the different aspects of law firm growth and management, membership in a mastermind or coaching group can be a truly worthwhile investment. Joining a mastermind was a turning point for me, and it gave me a chance to see what other women were doing across the country. Up to that point, I did not have any models in my immediate circle for the type of law practice I wanted. It's okay if not everyone understands what you want to do. But it is important to find others who not only understand, but are doing the same thing as you.

TAKE CARE OF YOURSELF

We need to forge a new model on our own terms, and only then can we really have it all. So where does self-care fit into all of this? You need to learn to take very good care of yourself. Download *We Should All Be Millionaires* and listen to it in the car, while you work out, or anytime you need a reminder that you deserve to take *really* good care of yourself. Reject the myth that mothers need to be martyrs, and that any time spent on ourselves is selfish.

What are some things that you want to start doing? What are some luxuries that would make you feel healthier, more relaxed, or more cared for? If you struggle with mom guilt, or you've convinced yourself you don't need, don't deserve, or can't afford something, try again. Rodgers suggests an exercise where you make a list of the lifestyle you want (your dream house, kids' school, extracurriculars, vacations, everything) and price it out to see what you need to earn to make it happen. Make sure you put yourself on the list. You can get a nice massage each month for $200, right? That's *one* consultation. Maybe a nice weekend getaway? Maybe all you need is one [whatever type of service you offer].

You are now a business, and the sole source of your income. Your clients, your team, and your family rely on you. You're pretty damn important. Get in the habit of taking good care of yourself. This may require you to work on your own mindset, and it may be an adjustment for your family. It's not your moral responsibility to do everyone's laundry. It's not selfish to rely on your kids' other parent—or a babysitter, or a grandparent—and take some time to spend on yourself. If you have a partner, home and child responsibilities belong to *both* of you. If you are single, there are probably other people in your life who love your kids, or a babysitter who can take care of them and show them a good time while you take care of yourself.

This doesn't need to be a special event. You should build into your regular life pockets of time where you take care of your own physical and mental health. Some of this you can build into a normal school/work day, like taking a half or full day off on Fridays for yourself. Look at things you can outsource, and don't write that suggestion off because you feel like you can't afford it (*yet*). Start small and work your way up to delegating tasks elsewhere. If you can't afford a housekeeper (*yet*), try a biweekly cleaning service. Find a dry cleaner that offers wash-and-fold and take turns with your partner dropping off weekly laundry. Use a grocery delivery service.

As your business grows and you make more money, there will be more room for you to prioritize nice things (whatever that looks like to you). However, you need to start the mindset shift now, and get comfortable with the idea that you deserve to be happy and healthy, and those needs don't come secondary to other people's health and happiness. Your family needs to come to understand that you don't need to do everything to be a good mom and prove your love.

Once you have established the practice and lifestyle you wanted, what's next? I encourage you to maintain a growth mindset— continually think about how you can serve more clients, pursue larger goals, and earn more money.

CHAPTER 10

GROWING YOUR PRACTICE

Once you've launched your law firm, the next step is to chart your growth. In the very early days of your law firm, when you're wearing a dozen different hats and figuring things out, you may not feel balanced and relaxed. You may be wondering why you traded a steady job for even more responsibility and unpredictability. While entrepreneurship is a new challenge and carries a different type of stress, keep your eye on the prize. The key to building wealth and power in a balanced way is to grow and scale your firm. You won't be the person answering the phone, and drafting briefs, and running marketing campaigns for very long. I once heard a very successful lawyer say "you can't be the guy running things and also be the guy in court." You can't be the woman running a successful business and also be the woman returning voicemails and drafting pleadings. The degree and timing of growth will vary by law firm, depending on your individual goals. What I don't want is for you to remain small out of fear or lack of self-confidence. Growing your firm, if done properly, will translate to both more money and more flexibility—and to less time in the office, because you will have more support.

DELEGATING

If you are starting your practice with a financial cushion and some capital investment, you may be opening your doors with at least one team member. The key to scaling is to identify the most pressing needs and fill them in order. Team member roles are going to evolve. In the beginning, the first hire or two may be handling various different tasks. As revenue increases and you fill more roles, each position will become more focused and specialized. Beginning with part-time or virtual roles and then evolving the positions into full-time or in-office is a safe way to grow gradually. However, many people begin their practice as "true solos." If you are starting a firm completely from scratch, with no clients, you will probably be a true solo and do all the things initially. If you are hanging your shingle with an existing client list, you may be in a position to have a legal assistant, or at least some administrative help, right off the bat. Either way, you are going to grow and likely start thinking about hiring within the first six to twelve months.

Experts say to hire before it's desperate. You don't want to be backlogged on cases with deadlines looming and *then* try to hire (and train) a legal assistant. You don't want to wait until the phones are ringing off the hook and you're missing every other call and *then* look for a receptionist. Personally, I know it's time to hire when I just start feeling overwhelmed, or I find that I'm spending my time on things that aren't the best use of it. To help guide your hiring, try this exercise: list out all the tasks you do in a week. Then, next to each task, grade it on a scale of one to five, with one being the tasks you excel at, enjoy doing, and feel need to be done by *you* as the business owner, and five being the tasks that you do out of pure necessity but that could easily be delegated to others with little impact. For example:

TASKS

~~Return phone messages~~ 4

~~Open and sort mail~~ 5

(Meet with prospective clients) 1

~~Process payments~~ 4

~~Schedule hearings with court clerk~~ 5

(Legal research and draft pleadings) 2

(Plan out new marketing strategies) 1

(Film social media content for firm) 1

Look at the threes, fours, and fives on your list. These are tasks that are taking up your precious time—time that could be spent on growing your business and generating revenue. Ideally, you should spend your time on ones and twos. I suspect that for most of you, the top tasks to get off your plate first will be answering the phone, administrative tasks, scheduling, and billing. Your first hire may well be a receptionist/legal assistant, so you can delegate all of these administrative tasks to that person. Doing so will free up more of your time to handle consultations, legal work, and business development. I learned this exercise several years ago at a Crisp seminar, and I actually repeat it myself regularly. I recommend that you try it at least once a quarter.

YOUR FIRST HIRE

If you do the exercise above, you will probably find that your fours and fives are tasks that should be done by a legal assistant.[25] This position will likely be the first hiring need in a young practice for most practice areas. Here are just a few things a legal assistant can take off your plate: review and sort documents received from clients or in discovery, prepare forms and draft pleadings for your review, record requests, electronically file pleadings, and write reports to summarize issues. As your first hire, the role will also involve some non-legal administrative tasks, including managing your calendar, following up with consultations, sending invoices and processing payments, ordering office supplies, and returning client calls (answering non-legal questions, and scheduling calls with you only as needed). It sounds like a lot of work—and it is—but in a brand new practice, this can probably be a single role. As your client list grows and you have predictable revenue, you will make your second hire and take some of these tasks off your first hire's plate, reassigning them to someone else.

Imagine what you could do with your time if someone were handling these tasks for you. You could finish your legal work more efficiently (and earn your fee more quickly); handle more consultations per week; and dedicate more time to marketing, networking, and professional development. That is the key to building a profitable firm. Monitor how you are spending your time to ensure it is maximized on growth and revenue-earning activities. When you do this exercise quarterly, your next hiring step will become very clear each time. Because I learned and started using this exercise, I have always known just which position is next for our firm.

DIPPING YOUR TOES IN

Hiring is probably the single most intimidating aspect of firm ownership. Once you actually take the plunge and start a business, the next scariest step is hiring someone else. This is a new responsibility, and it is normal to worry about making payroll and keeping your commitment to that person. It *is* a big responsibility, and it should be managed with care. When I have followed the exercise above of identifying the exact role needed, the role has instantly contributed to revenue. If you are filling the right position needed in your firm, that role will pay for itself, in a sense. For example, hiring your first legal assistant will free up your time to take on more consultations, devote more time to marketing, and close out cases more quickly. This should almost immediately result in you earning fees more quickly and signing on new business. An employee should be an investment, not a cost.

A virtual contractor is a comparatively stress-free way to make an initial hire and can also be a strategic long-term addition to your firm. There are several virtual staffing companies in the United States that will train, vet, and place virtual positions such as legal assistant, marketing assistant, or receptionist. I have used Get Staffed Up, a virtual staffing company that caters to lawyers and bilingual positions. This can be a very measured and streamlined approach to hiring. The company facilitates interviews with candidates they have already vetted to a degree, and if you find a match for your firm, you pay a monthly fee to the staffing company. They handle all of the employment aspects of the relationship, so the only cost to you is the monthly payment to the staffing company and any software subscriptions you may need to purchase for the staffer. The cost for a full-time virtual staffer is significantly less than an in-person position because of favorable exchange rates, and the staffing company is the employer handling things like taxes and leave. I have successfully used this approach both for short-term solutions and for long-term additions to my firm. If you plan to use a virtual staffer, particularly internationally, I would *only* work with a reputable company to ensure that everything is handled properly and the staffer is being compensated appropriately.

VIRTUAL OR IN PERSON

We know that the COVID-19 pandemic forced many firms to close their physical offices and go virtual, and some firms are staying that way. As we discussed in the beginning, there are different considerations that support either having a physical office or a fully virtual office. In my practice areas, most firms saw a relatively early return to physical offices and a resumption of business as usual. While we continue to offer virtual consultations and meetings, and we can largely serve clients virtually, many clients prefer to come to the office. Our team also primarily prefers working in the office. We can be described as a hybrid. We have a full in-office staff complemented by several key positions held virtually. Currently, our intake, billing, and marketing are handled virtually, and our legal research and writing attorney positions are virtual. Personally, I see benefits to the physical office and have no plans to go fully virtual in the near future. However, if you are fully virtual and plan to stay that way, or if you see yourself as fitting the hybrid model, your hiring options expand, as well.

There are different considerations to training, managing, and supervising remote team members. With any team member, you need to ensure that you are maximizing their time efficiently. With virtual team members, you need to prioritize communication and metrics. At our firm, we have a full staff meeting every Monday for in-person and virtual staff to discuss open cases, deadlines, and any other office matters. It's important to both supervise and include virtual team members. Fortunately, there are many ways virtual and in-office teams can remain in sync. Some offices use programs like Slack or G-Chat to communicate throughout the day. I prefer to communicate primarily through our case management system so that all case-related communication is documented and in a central location. Chatting functions should be reserved for quick non-substantive questions or messages like "Your two o'clock appointment called. She is running late." I find that having regular face-time through video meetings using a program like Zoom or Google Meet is important.

COMPENSATION AND BENEFITS

When you hire your first full-time employee, whether virtual or in-person, you want to make sure that compensation is a priority. Remember, our goal is to make the legal profession more accessible for women to excel. We want to build wealth and power for ourselves and each other. When we invite others to "sit at our table," we need to walk the walk and be employers who nurture and reward excellence in the people who come and work with us. This means providing a good work environment, appropriate compensation, and benefits. If this sounds daunting and expensive, remember that employees should be an investment, not a cost. You want to make a good investment, and you will expect a positive return.

SALARY

Once you determine the position you need to fill, set a salary or salary range. Some firms compensate hourly. In my firm, every full-time position is salaried and works a thirty-six-hour work week. Do some market research in your area to assess what an appropriate salary range may be. This can be challenging because a lot of data is outdated, and many employers don't like to discuss compensation. Usually, you can find some data on comparable job titles. If you've worked for another firm or agency, you may have an idea of what support staff positions are paid. The logistics of payroll are made easy by various programs that automate the fees and taxes. We use Gusto, a payroll platform that schedules pay dates, pays the taxes, and syncs with our benefit plans.

PAID LEAVE

This is a benefit I feel very strongly about, and it's an opportunity for women business owners to show up. At our firm, every full time employee starts with five weeks of paid time off per year. According to 2021 government data, fewer than 2 percent of US employers offer this much leave to new employees.[26] I do not see any benefit in distinguishing between sick leave and vacation time, because we should be giving people an appropriate amount of paid leave to use as they need or want. Before you make your first hire, consider your own values and how they translate into what you offer employees. If we believe that the path to equality and success for women is increased accessibility in the workplace to balance work and home, we need to offer our employees the same accessibility. I have found through my own practice that it is possible to structure generous leave policies without sacrificing profit. I also believe that good leave policies help businesses attract and retain excellent employees.

RETIREMENT

It is very easy to offer affordable retirement plans to employees as a small business. Yes, it is a cost—but it is more accessible than many people realize. In 2021, 67 percent of US employees in the private sector had access to 401k plans.[27] There are programs designed for small businesses to set up 401k accounts for employees. I use one called Guideline, which syncs with our payroll platform. It is incredibly user-friendly, and individual employees can easily log on and monitor their accounts and adjust their contributions. The administrative fees themselves are nominal, and you can set a match. We offer a 4 percent match to employees after twelve months of service. Yes, again, this is a business cost—but we are viewing costs as investments. As we build our own wealth and security, we want to help our employees achieve the same. One of our goals is supporting others, especially other women, in building wealth. When calculating costs for future employees, consider a retirement plan and match.

HEALTH INSURANCE

Health and dental insurance is another important benefit to consider for your team. This can be a relatively considerable cost to plan for when hiring. Insurance agents can facilitate employer-offered insurance plans. Because we use a payroll platform that syncs with benefits, it is very user friendly. If you plan to use a platform like Gusto, see what kinds of benefits they can run through that platform. At our firm, we offer full health, vision, and dental insurance to all full-time employees at no cost to the employee. Again, offering great insurance is an investment to attract and retain top-tier members, and one way to support the people who are helping you run your business.

One of the most rewarding aspects of being a woman business owner is having the opportunity to pay it forward. We became entrepreneurs to serve ourselves and our families, but we also have a chance to work to revolutionize the legal field for others. I encourage you to enact progressive policies in your firm to support other working mothers. We can do this—and still be profitable.

CONCLUSION

As a mother of young children, I'm frequently called upon to mediate debates of extreme importance, such as whether crocodiles are brownish-green or greenish-brown, or whether the witch actually dies in the end of *Hansel and Gretel*. My youngest son is the embodiment of "frequently wrong, never in doubt" and mostly asks for—then promptly rejects—my input. My daughter, on the other hand, views me as the authority. At six, she's at this exquisite stage of growing into herself while still viewing me as omniscient and just. She knows that my office is a special place, and that people come to me to help them with their problems. She always defends my authority to her brother, saying solemnly, "Mom's a lawyer."

Remember why *you* wanted to start your own firm. From now on, you are in the driver's seat of your own career and life. You will make decisions to set the professional and financial course of your practice. You will determine the work culture and values of your firm. You will establish your practice to reflect who you are and what you want to do.

And finally, remember the life you want. You want financial security. You want professional fulfillment. You want to leave the office at three in the afternoon to take your kids to the park. You want to spend your weekends hiking or visiting museums, or doing arts and crafts, or watching movies and eating popcorn. You want to take longer vacations or have Fridays off. Think of what this will mean for you, for your family, and for your future happiness.

You've been working on someone else's terms. You've been compromising on your own happiness. You've been *doing* it all instead of *having* it all.

Not anymore. No more making yourself smaller to fit in a box someone else built for you. No more trying to get a seat at the table—because you have your own table. You're in charge now. You're a businesswoman and a law firm owner. It's *all* you, and you've got this.

BEFORE YOU GO

At this point, you've executed your plan and opened your doors. You are building a digital presence, you've learned the right way to handle intake and consultations, and you're starting to see some money come through the door. Maybe you're still a one- woman show, or maybe you're already working with some virtual staff. Pour yourself a glass of champagne, because you started a law firm.

Entrepreneurship is definitely a journey, not a destination. There are ups and downs, amazing months and challenging months. Both you and your law firm will always be evolving.

As you grow and learn, you will implement new ideas in your business. As your business grows, you will need to respond to new and different challenges. The more staff you hire, the more you need to pay attention to employment and human resource issues. The more revenue that flows in, the more complicated your firm finances will become. As your reputation grows, you may expand your practice areas. My advice is to never stop learning and growing. Entrepreneur Michael Mogill says, "never take your foot off the gas." What we are building are not *just* law firms. They are law firms for a modern age, businesses that serve *our* lives and *our* needs. We serve a purpose in our community, and we are forging businesses that allow us to excel at work *and* be happy at home.

When women support other women, amazing things can happen. We can change laws, cultural norms, and economies. What I want for all of us is professional fulfillment, financial independence, and healthy home lives. I know that our ticket is building firms and changing the legal profession from the inside by demanding what we want and setting an example for others.

I created *Mom's A Lawyer* and developed the Law Firm Launch as an affordable comprehensive toolkit for women just embarking on law firm ownership. My mission is to support women—particularly mothers—as they found, grow, and scale law firms to fit their lives. The world of law firm management can be daunting. Without a basic foundation, it can be confusing to know how to evaluate different higher-level offerings. For more resources and community support, visit www.momsalawyer.com or follow along on social media @moms_a_lawyer.

REQUIRED READING AND LISTENING

FOR WOMEN ENTREPRENEURS AND WORKING MOMS:

- *We Should All Be Millionaires* by Rachel Rodgers
- *Chillpreneur* by Denise Duffield-Thomas
- *Entreprenista* Podcast
- *Oh Sh*t What Now* Podcast
- *What She Said* Podcast
- *LawHer* Podcast

FOR LAW FIRM OWNERS:

- *The Game-Changing Attorney* by Michael Mogill
- *Fireproof* by Michael Morse
- *The Lawyer As CEO* by Reza Torkzadeh
- *Hello Seven* Podcast
- *The Game-Changing Attorney* Podcast

- *The Law Entrepreneur* Podcast
- *The Lawyerist* Podcast

FOR ENTREPRENEURS:

- *Never Lose A Customer Again by* Joey Coleman
- *The Pumpkin Plan* by Mike Michalowicz

ACKNOWLEDGMENTS

I am so fortunate to have a supportive family. My parents, Alan and Roberta, were super-parents and are super-grandparents. My husband, Michael, is a true partner in everything we do. Our kids—Jack, June, and Jacob—are simply amazing. My team at Airington Law inspires me daily.

ABOUT THE AUTHOR

MIRIAM AIRINGTON-FISHER, the best-selling author of *Mom's A Lawyer: How to Start a Firm and Take Control of Your Life*, is an award-winning attorney and owner of Airington Law, a Virginia-based, women-led law firm specializing in civil rights, criminal defense, and immigration, and the founder of Mom's A Lawyer, a company dedicated to promoting accessibility for working mothers in the legal profession. Miriam co-hosts the *Accessory to Justice* Podcast and develops digital products designed to support women in building and growing progressive law firms. For more information, visit www.momsalawyer.com or follow her on social media at @moms_a_lawyer.

NOTES

1   Jane R. Bambauer and Tauhidur Rahman, "The Quiet Resignation: Why Do So Many Female Lawyers Abandon Their Careers?" *UC Irvine Law Review* 10, no. 3 (March 2020), https://scholarship.law.uci.edu/ucilr/vol10/iss3/5.

2   Justin Anker and Patrick R. Krill, "Stress, Drink, Leave: An Examination of Gender-Specific Risk Factors for Mental Health Problems and Attrition Among Licensed Attorneys," *PLoS ONE* 16, no. 5 (May 2021), https://doi.org/10.1371/journal.pone.0250563.

3   Clinton Global Initiative, "Empowering Girls & Women," accessed September 9, 2022, https://www.un.org/en/ecosoc/phlntrpy/notes/clinton.pdf.

4   Bambauer and Rahman, "The Quiet Resignation." See also Lois W. Hoffman and Lise M. Youngblade, Mothers at Work: Effects on Children's Well-Being (Cambridge, UK: Cambridge University Press, 1999); Kathleen L. McGinn, Mayra Ruiz Castro, and Elizabeth Long Lingo, "Learning from Mum: Cross National Evidence Linking Maternal Employment and Adult Children's Outcomes," Work, Employment and Society 33, no. 3 (2019), https://doi.org/10.1177/0950017018760167; Alyssa Croft et al., "The Second Shift Reflected in the Second Generation: Do Parents' Gender Roles at Home Predict Children's Aspirations?" Psychological Science 25, no. 7 (June 2014), https://doi.org/10.1177/0956797614533968.

5   Joyce Sterling and Linda Chanow, *In Their Own Words: Experienced Women Lawyers Explain Why They Are Leaving Their Law Firms and the Profession,* American Bar Association Commission on Women in the Profession (2021), https://www.americanbar.org/content/dam/aba/administrative/women/intheirownwords-f-4-19-21-final.pdf.

6   Bambauer and Rahman, "The Quiet Resignation."

7   Bambauer and Rahman, "The Quiet Resignation." See also David B. Wilkins, Bryon Fong, and Ronit Dinovitzer, "The Women and Men of Harvard Law School: The Preliminary Results from the HLS Career Study," HLS Center on the Legal Profession Research Paper No. 2015-6 (May 2015), https://doi.org/10.2139/ssrn.2609499; John Monahan and Jeffrey Swanson, "Lawyers at Mid-Career: A 20-Year Longitudinal Study of Job and Life Satisfaction," *Journal of Empirical Legal Studies* 6, no. 3 (August 2009), https://doi.org/10.1111/j.1740-1461.2009.01150.x.

8   Pooja Lakshmin, "How Society Has Turned Its Back on Mothers," *New York Times*, February 4, 2021, https://www.nytimes.com/2021/02/04/parenting/working-mom-burnout-coronavirus.html.

9   Caroline Spiezio, "Mental Health, Stress, Have One-in-Four Women Lawyers Mulling Career Change," Reuters, May 17 2021, https://www.reuters.com/business/legal/mental-health-stress-have-one-in-four-women-lawyers-mulling-career-change-2021-05-12.

10   Bambauer and Rahman, "The Quiet Resignation."

11   "For Both Moms and Dads, More Time Spent on Childcare," Pew Research Center, June 15, 2017, https://www.pewresearch.org/ft_17-06-14_fathers_1965_2015.

12   Stephanie Francis Ward, "More Female than Male Lawyers Are Engaging in Risky Drinking, New Study Finds," *ABA Journal*, May 12, 2021, https://www.abajournal.com/news/article/more-women-than-men-lawyers-engaging-in-risky-drinking-study-finds.

13   Jessica L. Borelli et al., "Gender Differences in Work-Family Guilt in Parents of Young Children," *Sex Roles* 76 (March 2017), https://doi.org/10.1007/s11199-016-0579-0.

14   Amy Joyce, "Ruth Bader Ginsburg Was the Model We Working Moms Needed," *Washington Post*, September 19, 2020, https://www.washingtonpost.com/lifestyle/2020/09/19/ruth-bader-ginsburg-working-mom-icon.

15   Bates v. State Bar of Arizona, 433 U.S. 350 (1977), https://supreme.justia.com/cases/federal/us/433/350/.

16   "Global Social Media Statistics," Data Reportal, accessed September 9, 2022, https://datareportal.com/social-media-users.

17   John Gramlich, "10 Facts About Americans and Facebook," Pew Research Center, June 1, 2021, https://www.pewresearch.org/fact-tank/2021/06/01/facts-about-americans-and-facebook.

18   Gramlich, "10 Facts About Americans and Facebook."

19   Gramlich, "10 Facts About Americans and Facebook."

20 "Social Media Fact Sheet," Pew Research Center, April 7, 2021, https://www.pewresearch.org/internet/fact-sheet/social-media/?menuItem=c14683cb-c4f4-41d0-a635-52c4eeae0245.

21 Meltem Odabaş, "10 Facts About Americans and Twitter," Pew Research Center, May 5, 2022, https://www.pewresearch.org/fact-tank/2019/08/02/10-facts-about-americans-and-twitter.

22 "Who Uses TikTok, Nextdoor," Pew Research Center, April 7, 2021, https://www.pewresearch.org/internet/chart/who-uses-tiktok-nextdoor.

23 Board of Governors of the Federal Reserve System, "Survey of Household Economics and Decisionmaking," updated May 23, 2022, https://www.federalreserve.gov/consumerscommunities/shed_data.htm.

24 We require pay in full for certain emergency cases or cases with a relatively small fee. For example, if someone hires us right before a filing deadline, we are going to need to prioritize their case and file quickly. In that situation, we typically require the fee to be paid in full because the fee is going to be earned very quickly. Similarly, if someone hires us for a very limited purpose or something that is a fairly small fee relative to our other work, we do not offer a payment plan.

25 The Bureau of Labor Statistics Occupational Outlook Handbook does not distinguish between job roles of legal assistant and paralegal. In my firm, a paralegal has more responsibility to draft legal arguments and identify potential issues (subject to attorney review and supervision) while a legal assistant supports the paralegal role and handles general administrative tasks.

26 US Bureau of Labor Statistics, "Who Receives Paid Vacations?" Employee Benefits Survey, modified September 23, 2021, https://www.bls.gov/ncs/ebs/factsheet/paid-vacations.htm.

27 U.S. Bureau of Labor Statistics, "67 Percent of Private Industry Workers Had Access to Retirement Plans in 2020," *The Economics Daily*, March 1, 2021, https://www.bls.gov/opub/ted/2021/67-percent-of-private-industry-workers-had-access-to-retirement-plans-in-2020.htm.